A Different Spirit:
*The Jewish Theological Seminary
of America, 1886-1902*

*This volume has been published with the generous
support of Natalie and Murray S. Katz, New York City.*

A Different Spirit:
The Jewish Theological Seminary of America, 1886-1902

Robert E. Fierstien

THE JEWISH THEOLOGICAL SEMINARY OF AMERICA
New York   1990/5750

AND THE BUSH הסנה
WAS NOT איננו
CONSUMED אכל

A Different Spirit:
The Jewish Theological Seminary of America, 1886-1902

Robert E. Fierstien

Library of Congress Cataloging in Publication Data

Fierstien, Robert E.
   A different spirit : the Jewish Theological Seminary of America.
   1886-1902 / Robert E. Fierstien.
        p.   cm.
   "A revision of my doctoral dissertation . . . Jewish Theological
   Seminary of America" --P.
   Includes bibliographical references.
   1. Jewish Theological Seminary of America--History. 2. Judaism-
   -Study and teaching (Higher)--United States--History--19th century.
   I. Title.
   ISBN 0-87334-064-7 (alk. paper). ISBN 0-87334-063-9 (pbk. : alk. paper)
   BM90.J4F54 1990
   296.8'342'0973--dc20   89-71732
                                                             CIP

Printed in the United States of America
on acid-free paper

In the new Seminary a different spirit will prevail, different impulses will pervade its teachings and animate its teachers. This spirit shall be that of Conservative Judaism, the conserving Jewish impulse which will create in the pupils of the Seminary the tendency to recognize the dual nature of Judaism and the Law; which unites theory and practice, identifies body and the soul, realizes the importance of both matter and spirit, and acknowledges the necessity of observing the Law as well as studying it.

—Alexander Kohut, January 2, 1887.

For Ruth and Jeremy,
With Love

CONTENTS

PREFACE

As the Jewish Theological Seminary of America enters its second century, it is important to look to its past, as well as to its future. Founded in 1886 as an alternative to the Reform Hebrew Union College, the Seminary has grown to become the spiritual and intellectual center of the religious movement known as Conservative Judaism. Despite the tremendous importance of the Seminary to the history of Judaism in America, however, no serious study of the early days of the institution has ever been written. Indeed, most general American Jewish history books begin their discussion of the Seminary with the arrival of Solomon Schechter in 1902, and make scarcely any mention of the early period. Even the excellent and serious treatments of the early history of Conservative Judaism by Moshe Davis, Herbert Parzen, and Herbert Rosenblum confine themselves largely to the founding and reorganization of the Seminary, and do not attempt to describe the everyday functioning of the Seminary as an academic institution.

To some degree, this situation is to be explained by the almost complete lack of primary material from the early Seminary itself: roll books, teachers' reports, student notes—all these have been largely lost through the passage of time, or scattered so widely as to make them virtually inaccessible. The Seminary Archives, the Drachman Collection at Yeshiva University, the American Jewish Archives at Cincinnati, all have very little archival material pertaining to the early Seminary. Although the Morais Collection at the Annenberg Research Institute does contain some excellent material, much of it applies only to the very earliest years of the Seminary's existence. Nevertheless, there is one excellent and comprehensive source for the early Seminary that is still in existence, and that is the pages of the *American Hebrew*. Founded in 1879, by a group of Jewish community activists who shared the moderate traditional outlook of the early Seminary, the *American Hebrew* quickly became a leading proponent of the Seminary from the days of its very inception; and it has provided us with a thorough running account of the daily activities of the early institution. By utilizing the weekly reports of the *American Hebrew*, we have been able to piece together the story of the early Seminary in a manner that is possible from no other source.

Our purpose in this study, therefore, is to describe the functioning of the Jewish Theological Seminary from its foundation in 1886 until its reorganization in 1902. It is hoped that this work will demonstrate that the early Seminary was a first-rate academic institution from its inception, many of whose graduates went on to careers of distinction and prestige in the rabbinate; and it is also hoped that we will demonstrate that, long before the arrival of Solomon Schechter, the Jewish Theological Seminary played a vital and significant role in the intellectual and religious life of the Jews in America.

ACKNOWLEDGMENTS

I would like to take this opportunity to thank the many individuals who helped in the preparation of this work, which is a revision of my doctoral dissertation, as well as the institutions who graciously permitted me to use their facilities. My deepest appreciation and gratitude go to my doctoral advisor, Dr. Ismar Schorsch, Chancellor of the Jewish Theological Seminary of America, for his guidance, inspiration, patience, and encouragement. I would like to thank Dr. Jack Wertheimer for serving as a reader for the original dissertation, and for his many helpful suggestions. In addition, I would like to gratefully acknowledge the help and guidance of the following individuals: Rabbi Jonathan Waxman, for his many suggestions and for reading part of the manuscript; Rabbi Joseph Brodie, for his constant encouragement and advice; and Rabbi Simon Noveck, for helping in the general organization of the work. Many thanks also go to Professor Abraham J. Karp, Professor Marc Lee Raphael, and Professor Pamela S. Nadell for their wise and useful suggestions, to Professor Jeffrey S. Gurock for sharing his knowledge of the Jewish Endeavor Society, and to Rabbi Stanley Rabinowitz for providing me with material on Adolphus S. Solomons.

Dr. John S. Ruskay, Vice-Chancellor of the Seminary, guided the entire publication project with great enthusiasm, earning my most sincere appreciation. Ms. Jean Highland, the Seminary's wonderful and expert Publications Consultant, was a constant source of encouragement and assistance to me throughout all the stages of publication, and I am deeply grateful to her. Many thanks also go to Dr. Mayer Rabinowitz, Librarian of the Seminary, and to Ms. Evelyn Cohen, Curator of Jewish Art at the Seminary Library, for help in selecting the illustrations for this volume. At Scholars Press, Dr. Harry Gilmer, Dr. Dennis Ford, and Mr. Darwin Melnyk were extremely helpful to me, and I wish to thank them for their efforts.

I would also like to thank the very able library staffs of the following institutions: The Jewish Theological Seminary of America, Hebrew Union College-Jewish Institute of Religion, Yeshiva University, Dropsie University (now the Annenberg Research Institute), Drew University, the American Jewish Archives, the American Jewish Historical Society, and the American Jewish Periodical Center. A special note of thanks goes to the wonderful library staff of Georgian Court College, Lakewood, New Jersey, who graciously allowed me to use their microfilm facilities.

The officers and members of my congregation, Temple Beth Or, Brick, New Jersey, were extraordinarily understanding and encouraging to me, and I wish to thank all of them, especially the president, Mrs. Marlene Lesk, and the past president, Mr. Arthur Stoll, during whose term the work was completed. I also want to thank Mrs. MaryLou Leask for her after-hours help in the production of various stages of this book.

My heartfelt appreciation and gratitude go to Natalie and Murray S. Katz of New York City for their devotion to Jewish scholarship and for their generous support of the publication of this volume.

Finally, it is my greatest pleasure to thank my wife, Ruth, and my son, Jeremy Israel, for their patience and encouragement. To them this work is dedicated with love.

R.E.F.
October 1989

Chapter I

Introduction

T he era which gave birth to the Jewish Theological Seminary was a truly momentous one for American Jewry. From a post-Colonial community dominated by a Sephardic elite in the early 1800's, the Jewish community of the 1880's had grown substantially, and was now dominated by the newer German-Jewish element at the peak of their creative powers. Arriving largely in the four decades preceding the Civil War, the German Jews had rapidly adapted to American life,[1] engulfing the established Jewish community which could trace its origins back to the year 1654. From a tiny group of, perhaps, 2,500 Jews at the beginning of the nineteenth century, the Jewish community of the United States had grown to over a quarter of a million souls by 1880. Even more important, the massive Jewish immigration from Eastern Europe, particularly Russia, was just beginning in the 1880's, the result of the hostility, persecution, discrimination, and economic dislocation which they endured in their native land. In the 1880's alone, more than 200,000 Jews came to the United States from Eastern Europe,[2] just a fraction of the almost two and one-half million that were to arrive by 1925.

When the immigrants of the 1880's arrived, they found a broad variety of religious expression, which can only loosely be categorized into two groups, Orthodox and Reform. The truth of the matter is that there was a wide spectrum of religious practice and belief on the part of both laymen and rabbis. The leading Reform rabbi of the time was Isaac Mayer Wise of Cincinnati (1819-1900). Born in

---

[1]Naomi W. Cohen, *Encounter with Emancipation; The German Jews in the United States 1830-1914* (Phila., 1984), pp. 12-14.

[2]George M. Price, "The Russian Jews In America," trans. Leo Shpall, in Abraham J. Karp, ed., *The Jewish Experience in America*, (N.Y./Waltham, 1969), Vol. IV, pp. 269-270.

Bavaria, Wise had been a rabbi in Radnitz, Bohemia, before coming to America in 1846, after which he served as rabbi in Albany, New York, and moved to Cincinnati in 1853. Although he was not a radical by choice or by temperament, Wise slowly began to disseminate the Reform ideology he had been exposed to in Germany, principally through the medium of his newspapers, *The Israelite* (later called *The American Israelite*) and *Die Deborah*; and, in so doing, he joined the ranks of pioneering Reformers such as Max Lilienthal, Leo Merzbacher, and, later, David Einhorn.

Wise's efforts to fashion what he termed a *Minhag America*, a form of Judaism which would be in harmony with American values, sensibilities, and aesthetics, slowly paid off, for, as Leon A. Jick has noted, "by 1870 . . . there were few congregations in America in which substantial reforms had *not* been introduced and in which an accelerating program of radical revision was *not* in process."[3] In 1873, Wise had been instrumental in founding the Union of American Hebrew Congregations, and two years later he founded the Hebrew Union College. Wise was by far not the most radical of Reform rabbis in the 1880's. Further to the left were men such as Kaufmann Kohler, David Einhorn's son-in-law, who disagreed violently with Wise on issues such as Sunday services, which Kohler condoned, and Biblical criticism.

To the right of Wise were men such as Alexander Kohut of New York, Marcus Jastrow of Philadelphia, and Benjamin Szold of Baltimore. These rabbis, particularly Kohut and Szold, were not hostile to reforms in Judaism; and they each participated in a radical revision of the *siddur*, eliminating such traditional concepts as the sacrifices and the resurrection of the dead, and incorporating large amounts of English into the service.[4] Nevertheless, on issues such as kashruth and the Sabbath, they supported the traditional point of view; and they each rejected the openly Reform position represented by Isaac Mayer Wise and the Hebrew Union College.

---

[3]Leon A. Jick, *The Americanization of the Synagogue 1820-1870* (Hanover, N.H., 1976), p. 174.

[4]See Alexander Kohut trans., *Prayers for the Divine Service of Congregation Ahawath Chesed*, arr. by Dr. A. Huebsch (N.Y., 1889), and also Benjamin Szold, Marcus Jastrow, and Henry Hochheimer, *Avodat Yisrael, Israelitish Prayer Book for All The Services of The Year* (Phila., 1885).

Further to the right were the avowed traditionalists, who followed in the footsteps of the great Isaac Leeser (1806-1868). Having come to America from his native Germany in 1824, Leeser was elected *hazzan* of the Sephardic Congregation Mickve (now Mikveh) Israel in Philadelphia in 1829, thereby beginning a long and multi-faceted career as the acknowledged leader of traditional American Jewry.[5] Leeser pioneered in almost every field of Jewish endeavor in the United States, translating the Bible and the *siddur* into English, writing textbooks for American Jewish children, and publishing a newspaper, The *Occident and American Jewish Advocate*,[6] in which he displayed a strongly traditionalist point of view. Leeser and Wise tried in vain to bridge their differences, principally at the Cleveland Conference of 1855;[7] but, in the long run, the theological gap between the two men proved too wide, and American Jewry could not be united. After the passing of Leeser, the leadership of traditional American Jewry fell to Sabato Morais of Philadelphia, who was later joined by men such as Henry Pereira Mendes of New York, and Bernard Drachman of Newark and, later, New York. These men did not reject the adjective "orthodox," and they saw as their primary rabbinical role the maintenance and preservation of the Jewish tradition in America.

Although Moshe Davis has included these men along with Kohut, Szold, and Jastrow in the movement that he terms the "Historical School,"[8] it is important to note, as Davis does, that the "School" comprised a definite right and left wing. On issues such as prayerbook revision, family pews, organ music, and English in the service, there was an enormous gap between the two groups that Davis has postulated as constituting the "Historical School." Still, there was some recognition of commonality, for in a sermon delivered in the mid-1880's, Morais praised Kohut as a "co-laborer" and

---

[5]Moshe Davis, *The Emergence of Conservative Judaism: The Historical School in 19th Century America* (Phila., 1965), pp. 347-349.

[6]Maxwell Whiteman, "Isaac Leeser and the Jews of Philadelphia," in *The Jewish Experience In America*, Vol. 3, p. 40.

[7]Isaac Mayer Wise, *Reminiscences*, trans. David Philipson (N.Y., 1945), p. 314.

[8]Davis, *Emergence*, pp. 14-20.

as a true "Conservative Rabbi";[9] and he harbored similar warm feelings towards Jastrow and Szold, who became supporters of the Seminary.

Although Morais, Pereira Mendes, and Drachman, among others, saw themselves as "orthodox," the type of Western European orthodoxy that they practiced was very different from that of the immigrants from Eastern Europe. The first Eastern European orthodox congregation in America, the Beth Hamedrash, had been founded in New York City in 1852,[10] but it was not until the immigration wave of the 1880's that large numbers of Eastern European orthodox Jews began to settle in the United States. In 1887, Rabbi Moses Weinberger estimated that there were 130 orthodox synagogues in New York alone, 240 including the smaller *shtieblach*, and over 300, counting private *minyanim* meeting in houses.[11] Most of these *shuls* were poor and lacked adequate rabbinic leadership. Often, the services were led by a non-ordained "reverend," and educational facilities for the young were almost completely lacking. Even among the larger congregations of the Lower East Side, very little emphasis was placed upon rabbinic learning; instead, they would often spend extravagant sums to attract famous *hazzanim* to grace their services. As Weinberger noted, "the modern tanners, the unworthy generation that has merited to bask in the light of America, prefer a sweet-singing *chazan* to all the rabbis, judges, preachers, and expositors in the world."[12] Even greater problems for Judaism were caused by the fact that many Jews of the ghetto worked such long hours that they had no time for Jewish observance; and, in addition, the younger generation was often repelled by the alien, un-American, Yiddish culture of their parents.

The question often arises as to whether the American Jewish community of the 1880's witnessed the tripartite division that we

---

[9]Sabato Morais, sermon, "On the Ministerial Conference at Baltimore," n.d., Morais Papers, Annenberg Research Institute.

[10]Judah David Eisenstein, "The History of the First Russian-American Jewish Congregation," in *The Jewish Experience In America*, Vol. 3, p. 141.

[11]Jonathan D. Sarna, trans. and ed., *People Walk on Their Heads, Moses Weinberger's 'Jews and Judaism in New York'* (N.Y., 1982), p. 40.

[12]Ibid., p. 42.

take for granted in the twentieth century—Reform, Conservative, and Orthodox Judaism. In general, traditionalists such as Morais used the words "orthodox" and "conservative" interchangeably. Nevertheless, among the Eastern European orthodox, the term "conservative" was indeed used, in almost the very same sense that it is employed today. Thus, in an 1886 article critical of the founding of the Seminary, J. D. Eisenstein wrote, "Judaism in America is divided into three classes or parties; Orthodox, Conservative, and Radical";[13] and the same distinction was made by Rabbi Moses Weinberger in his *HaYehudim Vi-haYahadut b'New York*:

> As we see it, dear readers, all the new parties have the same value; only two or three inches separate them. Ultimately they will all unite, for a single spirit binds them. We do not believe that American Judaism can hope for much, not from the radicals, the conservatives, the liberals, nor even from those who have just recently begun to alter their ways.[14]

In mentioning the Conservatives, Eisenstein not only included Alexander Kohut, who served in a synagogue that was very close to Reform, but also Sabato Morais, because he said publicly that he did not desire the restoration of the sacrifices after the Temple is rebuilt.[15]

This, then, was the Jewish world of the 1880's into which the Seminary was born. On the top of the social scale (in their eyes) were the German Jewish community and the remnants of the early Sephardic settlement, along with other Western European Jews— Dutch, English, etc.—who had become highly Americanized and wanted a Judaism, whether traditional or Reform, that would harmonize well with their perception of American values, mores and sense of decorum. At the other end of the social scale were the recent immigrants from Eastern Europe, still a somewhat smaller community than the first, but growing rapidly day by day. To the

---

[13]Judah David Eisenstein, "Yesod HaSeminar HeHadash," in *Ozar Zikhronothai: Autobiography and Memoirs* (N.Y., 1929), p. 206; reprinted from the *New Yorker Yidishe Zeitung*, 1886.

[14]Sarna, *People Walk*, p. 65.

[15]Eisenstein, "Yesod," p. 209.

older Jewish community, the immigrants were an embarrassment or even a nuisance: with their Yiddish language, their old-fashioned dress, and their cacophonous style of worship, the new arrivals were often seen as a threat by the older community, who felt that they might stir up anti-Semitism and resentment against all Jews. To Americanize the immigrants became a top priority for the older community, and the Seminary was destined to play a great role in this process. Although the Seminary was founded almost exclusively by the older Jewish community, it was to the new arrivals that the Seminary would ultimately turn in its struggle for survival, as well as for success.

Before we deal with the conditions and events which led to the founding of the Seminary in 1886, we would do well to take a brief look at the history of higher Jewish education in America up to that time. In the Colonial period, the level of Jewish knowledge was generally very low, and the possibilities for higher Jewish education were almost non-existent. Most of the early *hazzanim* had received their training elsewhere; and even the most famous Colonial *hazzan*, Gershom Mendes Seixas, who was born and educated in New York, was largely self-taught in Jewish matters. As the American Jewish community began to grow in the early decades of the nineteenth century, the need for advanced Jewish education became apparent to all concerned observers. In May, 1821, at the urging of Moses Elias Levy of Florida, the Rev. M.L.M. Peixotto of Congregation Shearith Israel in New York, along with Mordecai Manuel Noah and Judah Zuntz, issued a circular proposing to establish "a Jewish institution of higher education," which would include a settlement and an agricultural school as well.[16] The plan came to naught, but the well-known Major Noah took up the idea and spoke about it frequently in many of the addresses he was called upon to give as New York's leading Jewish citizen.

---

[16]Bertram Wallace Korn, *Eventful Years And Experiences: Studies in Nineteenth Century American Jewish History* (Cincinnati, 1954), p. 152.

Pioneering in almost every constructive endeavor in the American Jewish community, Isaac Leeser also took up the cause of establishing a seminary early in his rabbinic career. As Bertram W. Korn has noted, as part of his 1841 proposal for a congregational union, Leeser, "appears to have been the first to campaign for the establishment of an educational institution created primarily for the training of young men as rabbis."[17] Although the proposed union was never organized, Leeser continued to use the pages of *The Occident* in the 1840's and 1850's to call for the establishment of a rabbinical and teachers' seminary. In 1849, at the request of Isaac Leeser, the Pennsylvania Legislature issued a charter to the Hebrew Education Society of Philadelphia to enable it to further Jewish education and to establish a rabbinical seminary; but once again, although the Society was founded and did proceed to improve the level of elementary Jewish education in Philadelphia, the seminary did not materialize.

In 1852, the well-known New York Jewish philanthropist, Sampson Simson, a founder of Mt. Sinai Hospital, resolved to establish a "Jewish Theological Seminary and Scientific Institute." Simson appointed a board of trustees for the institution, and gave four and one-half acres of land in Yonkers upon which to build the school. Nevertheless, despite the auspicious beginning, Simson's proposal was never realized; and on May 10, 1888, by an act of the New York State Legislature, the paper Institute formally merged with the Jewish Theological Seminary, which held the Yonkers property for a number of years and finally sold it.[18]

Isaac Mayer Wise also perceived the need for the establishment of an institution to train American rabbis; and, like Isaac Leeser, he used the pages of his newspapers to further the proposal. In 1855, Wise organized the Zion Collegiate Association in Cincinnati, and then travelled around the country seeking to rally support for the opening of a Jewish college. As he later noted in his *Reminiscences,* "the plan was to organize similar associations in all the cities of the country, and then to have the united societies found and support a

---

[17]Ibid., p. 154.

[18]Solomon Solis Cohen, "The Jewish Theological Seminary, Past and Future," address delivered at the 1918 J.T.S. Commencement (N.Y., 1919), pp. 30-31.

higher Jewish academy or college."[19] Chapters were eventually
opened in Louisville, Cleveland, New York, and Baltimore, as well
as in Cincinnati; but only the Louisville and Cincinnati branches
were effective in raising money. Nevertheless, after a gala inaugural
banquet, at which Governor Salmon P. Chase was present, the
school opened in the fall of 1855, with "fourteen students, two of
whom were Christians, and five professors," including Wise and
Max Lilienthal.[20]

A glorified day school, Zion College taught both secular and religious subjects; but Wise's ultimate goal was to establish a rabbinical and pedagogical department.[21] Unfortunately, the school lan-
guished for lack of financial support; and just two years after its
founding, it closed its doors in 1857.[22] Writing many years later,
Wise asserted that "the people in Cincinnati" had pressured him
into opening the College prematurely: "This was done against my
will and intention; for nothing had as yet been accomplished outside
of this city to assume the permanence of such an institution ... I was
outvoted and persuaded, and permitted myself to be carried along
by the current."[23] Whatever the reality of the school's demise, Zion
College taught Isaac Mayer Wise the same lesson that Maimonides
College was to teach the traditionalists in the next decade—that in
order to succeed, any American rabbinical seminary would have to
be well-grounded financially and socially, as well as academically.

From the start, the Eastern Radical Reform rabbis had refused to
participate in Wise's Zion College project. In October, 1865, the two
leading Radical Reform rabbis of New York, Samuel Adler of
Temple Emanu-El and David Einhorn of Temple Beth El, founded
the "Emanu-El Theological Seminary Association." The Association,
which lasted for many years, had a rather interesting and varied history. Originally, it provided scholarships for prospective rabbinical
students at Columbia University. Later on, the Association provided

[19]Wise, *Reminiscences*, p. 285.
[20]Ibid., p. 324.
[21]David Philipson, *Centenary Papers And Others* (Cincinnati, 1919), p. 43.
[22]Michael A. Meyer, "A Centennial History," in Samuel E. Karff, ed., *Hebrew Union College-Jewish Institute of Religion At One Hundred Years* (Cincinnati, 1976), p. 15.
[23]Wise, *Reminiscences*, p. 305.

funds to send rabbinical students, such as Felix Adler and Emil G. Hirsch, to Germany to pursue their studies.

In 1877, the Association actually opened a preparatory school which, it was hoped, would ultimately provide rabbinical training. Among the faculty members were Rabbis Samuel Adler, Adolph Huebsch, Moses Mielziner, and Gustav Gottheil; and within a few years, it had approximately thirty students, several of whom, such as Samuel Schulman, Maurice Harris, and Bernard Drachman, went on to distinguished careers in the American rabbinate.[24]

Meeting in Milwaukee in 1878, the Union of American Hebrew Congregations decided that the Emanu-El Seminary should become a preparatory school for the Hebrew Union College. The school met on weekday afternoons and Sunday mornings, and attempted to provide a solid grounding in Bible, Talmud, Hebrew Grammar, and Jewish Philosophy; and the students were especially fortunate when the faculty secured the services of Arnold Ehrlich, who went on to a distinguished career as a Biblical scholar.[25] Despite the fact that the Union paid half of its budget, the New York school sent only a few students on to Cincinnati, and in 1885, it closed its doors.[26] For a number of years thereafter, the Association continued to exist, and provided scholarships for students at the Hebrew Union College.

In 1866, the year after the Emanu-El Association was founded, the B'nai B'rith organization also considered founding a Jewish university for the purpose of training rabbis and Jewish teachers. At the urging of its Grand Saar, Benjamin F. Peixotto, the Order passed a resolution at its annual convention in Cincinnati in October, 1866, calling for the establishment of such an institution. Each of the 7,000 members of B'nai B'rith was to contribute ten dollars, and each lodge was to contribute at least $500. Nevertheless, realizing the immensity of the task, in August, 1867, the Constitution Grand Lodge voted not to pursue the project.[27]

Not to be outdone by the Reformers, who had founded the Zion College in 1855, and, later, the Emanu-El Theological Seminary

---

[24]Richard Gottheil, *The Life of Gustav Gottheil: Memoir of a Priest in Israel* (Williamsport, Pa., 1936), p. 39.

[25]*American Hebrew (AH)*, Oct. 8, 1880, p. 93.

[26]Meyer, "Centennial History," pp. 40-41.

[27]Korn, *Eventful Years*, pp. 162-163.

Association in 1865, the traditionalists also tried to establish a rabbinical school in the middle of the nineteenth century. In November, 1864, Isaac Leeser assembled a group of wealthy Philadelphia laymen, including Abraham Hart and Moses A. Dropsie, and encouraged them to establish Maimonides College, for the purpose of training traditional American rabbis. The aid of other Philadelphia rabbis and the Hebrew Education Society was enlisted, and the school was opened in October, 1867. Among the first officers and trustees of the college were Hart, Dropsie, Mayer Sulzberger, and Myer S. Isaacs; and the institution also had the active backing of the Rev. S. M. Isaacs of New York, editor of the *Jewish Messenger*.

As originally intended, the college was to provide a full secular studies program, as well as Judaica courses in Bible, Talmud, Codes, Jewish History, Literature, and Philosophy. The faculty also was impressive: Leeser taught Homiletics, "Belles Lettres," and Comparative Theology; Rev. Sabato Morais taught Bible; Rev. Marcus Jastrow taught Talmud, Philosophy, Jewish History, and Literature; Rev. A.S. Bettelheim—later to become the father-in-law of Alexander Kohut—taught Mishnah, Shulchan Aruch, and Mishneh Torah; and the Rev. L. Buttenweiser taught Hebrew and "Chaldaic" Language.[28] Students had to be at least fourteen years of age; and as the official announcement for the opening of the college declared, "candidates for admission must be able to translate with facility the historical portions of the Bible."[29] Nevertheless, despite the high hopes of its founders, Maimonides College never succeeded. For one thing, very few students ever applied for admission. The College opened with only five students, and but three of them returned for the second year. In addition, Isaac Leeser died in 1868, and the institution was left without its guiding light. Sabato Morais and Marcus Jastrow struggled bravely to keep the school going, but their time was necessarily limited; and hampered by a lack of funds, students, and library facilities, Maimonides College closed in 1873, without having graduated a single rabbi.[30]

---

[28]Ibid., p. 166.

[29]Ibid., p. 167.

[30]The three students remaining at the end did, however, pursue successful careers in Judaica. David Levy and Samuel Mendelsohn entered the rabbinate, and Marcus Lam became a Hebrew teacher. Years later, Lam would become a

From an objective point of view, therefore, Maimonides College was a failure. Nevertheless, it must surely have served to teach Sabato Morais many a valuable lesson when he founded the Jewish Theological Seminary, more than a decade later. From the beginning, the Seminary was greatly concerned with building the kind of grass-roots support that Maimonides College lacked, through the development of local Seminary Association branches in various cities. Morais clearly understood the need for full-time faculty members and for an accessible library facility; and the fact that he chose New York rather than his own Philadelphia for the location of the Seminary is very likely a reflection of the disappointment that he felt in the apathy which led to the closing of Maimonides College.

Two years after the dissolution of Maimonides College, the Hebrew Union College was opened in Cincinnati in October, 1875, by the Union of American Hebrew Congregations, with Isaac Mayer Wise as its first president. Unlike the earlier Zion College, the Hebrew Union College sought to teach only Judaica. Students were required to attend either the public high schools or the university during the morning while studying at the Union College, as it was called, in the afternoon.[31] The school opened with nine students, four more were added during the first year, including one young lady; and most of them were native-born Americans. Many of them were very young: David Philipson relates how he entered the first class when he was but thirteen years of age.[32] At first, there were only two faculty members, Isaac Mayer Wise and Solomon Eppinger, "a local scholar and teacher who received the munificent salary of seven hundred dollars per annum";[33] but in the middle of the first year, Rev. Max Lilienthal joined the staff as well.

The students in the school's first year had a truly varied curriculum. They studied Humash, Psalms, Hebrew Grammar, Pirke Avot, parts of the Mechilta, Mishnah Sanhedrin and Sota with Bartenura,

---

regular contributor to the Seminary, and Mendelsohn would become an outspoken opponent of Isaac Mayer Wise (see letter from Mendelsohn to S. Morais, Jan. 15, 1884, in Morais Papers).

[31]David Philipson, "The History of the Hebrew Union College," in *Hebrew Union College Jubilee Volume (1875-1925)* (Cincinnati, 1925), p. 21.

[32]Ibid., p. 21.

[33]Ibid., p. 25.

and Jewish History. Every year for seven more years, a new class was added on to the school, making four grades in the Preparatory Department and four in the Collegiate Department. During the second year of the institution, the students began to study the Talmud, Tractate Berachot; and in September, 1879, the Collegiate Department first opened. In that same year, Moses Mielziner, who later became a well-known Talmud scholar, joined the faculty, serving until 1903. Essentially, the curriculum of the College was a highly traditional one in its early years. The students studied Bible, Hebrew and Aramaic Grammar, Mishnah, Gemara, Midrash, Codes, Philosophy, Theology, Jewish History, and Homiletics.[34]

Having learned from his Zion College experience the importance of securing a firm financial base for any institution of learning, Isaac Mayer Wise made fund-raising a top priority for the College. The school started out with a gift of $10,000 from Henry Adler of Lawrenceberg, Indiana, plus an additional $5,000 from the Union of American Hebrew Congregations, which was a rather small amount, considering the fact that the Union had seventy-two member congregations by 1875.[35] Nevertheless, Isaac Mayer Wise launched a vigorous campaign to raise funds, and by December, 1875, the school had received $64,000 in pledges. Compared to the puny sums raised for the Seminary in the 1880's and 1890's, the amounts donated to the early Hebrew Union College were large indeed. Initially, Isaac Mayer Wise had to contend with the opposition of the Eastern Radical Reformers, who sought to maintain the Emanu-El Seminary as an independent institution; but at the 1878 convention of the Union, held in Milwaukee, the two sides worked out their differences, and a united Reform support for the Hebrew Union College, both spiritually and financially, was assured.

One of the most interesting aspects of the early Hebrew Union College was the fact that it initially had the support of many of the leaders of traditional Judaism in America, such as Rabbis Sabato Morais, Marcus Jastrow, Benjamin Szold, and the learned Philadelphia layman, Mayer Sulzberger, all of whom served in vari-

---

[34]Ibid., p. 29; see also *AH*, July 2, 1880, p. 75.
[35]Meyer, "Centennial History," p. 18.

ous capacities to aid the new institution. Jastrow and Sulzberger, for example, were appointed at the U.A.H.C. Convention of 1878, to serve on a committee to set admission and degree standards for the College; and Benjamin Szold served as an examiner for the Public Examination of the school in 1883, and received an honorary Doctor of Divinity degree from the institution four years later.[36] Like Szold and Jastrow, Sabato Morais was an early supporter of the Union—although his synagogue steadfastly refused to join[37]—and he also helped the College by serving as an examiner in 1877 and 1878. In 1877, Morais was called upon to write the report for the board of examiners to the U.A.H.C.; and he declared that, "The general result of the examination proved very satisfactory. Taking into consideration that the students were engaged during the best hours of the day in secular studies at the Public Schools, the proficiency exhibited in various branches of sacred lore, exceeded, in many instances, the anticipation formed." After some suggestions for improvement, Morais concluded the report by asserting that, "The College at Cincinnati may unequivocally be pronounced an object deserving of the support of all Israelites."[38]

The questions obviously arise as to why the traditionalists, particularly Morais, were willing to support a college headed by an avowed Reformer like Isaac Mayer Wise, and why they were willing to participate in the affairs of the Union. For one thing, the traditionalists probably hoped to "capture" the Union, or at least to stem the tide of Reform which was so powerful in the 1870's; and in this hope, they were completely frustrated by the passage of time. In addition, Wise and his associates gave constant assurances that they had no intention of turning the College into a Reform institution; it was to be completely non-denominational, teaching only traditional Jewish law and lore. Thus, writing to Morais in 1877, Jacob Ezekiel, the Secretary of the College, asserted,

> Neither Dr. Wise or Dr. Lilienthal do *not* advance *their* ideas in contravention to the established opinions. . . We *are honest* and can do no

---

[36] Philipson, "History of H.U.C.," pp. 35, 67.
[37] See letter from Jacob Ezekiel to S. Morais, March 8, 1877, in Morais Papers.
[38] S. Morais, Report "To the Council of the Union of American Hebrew Congregations," 1877, Morais Papers.

more; I can say truly from what I have seen and heard at the classes that the minds of the students are not biased or hampered in any way, they are taught the Mishnah as it is, and when they arrive at a mature age, they . . . make their own deductions.[39]

As the school progressed, these assurances became meaningless; and the Hebrew Union College rapidly became an institution for the training of Reform rabbis.

There is one other explanation as to why Sabato Morais was willing to extend his support to the Hebrew Union College despite the fact that it was run by Isaac Mayer Wise: he hoped that it would somehow pave the way for the establishment of a traditional rabbinical seminary in Philadelphia. Writing to Morais in September, 1876, Wise lamented the fact that, "We have but two students from the East"; and he declared, "I believe that if the Philad. congregations come into the Union that the Maimonides College could be reopened as Preparatory, with four classes for four years."[40] The following March, Jacob Ezekiel wrote to Morais, holding out even more hope for the establishment of such an institution:

> I know full well your head and heart is [sic] with our cause, and I cannot expect you to use every influence with your congregation other than to speak a good word when needed [to raise funds for H.U.C.] . . . My main aim is to try and have the Eastern Preparatory School or Grades for the College proper located at Philadelphia, instead of New York, as Phila. for quietude is better adapted and I know you would be in your *element* to accomplish *that* towards our Union and College that you have always preferred.

Ezekiel then goes on to tell Morais that he would be welcome to teach at the Philadelphia school:

> As a matter of course, if you were to tender your services gratuitously for the first year or longer, as Dr. Wise has done, it might prove as a

---

[39]Letter from Jacob Ezekiel to S. Morais, March 8, 1877, Morais Papers.
[40]Letter from Wise to Morais, Sept. 15, 1876, Morais Papers.

stimulus to locate the Auxiliary at Phila. rather than pay a large salary to any one in New York.[41]

The following year, in September, 1878, Ezekiel once again wrote to Morais:

> I am pleased to learn that an effort will be made in Phila. to rear an advanced class of boys in the routine of our preparatory grade, that may be put under the auspices of our Union next year. I like to see the rivalry between Phila. and New York.[42]

Nevertheless, this was already after the 1878 U.A.H.C. convention in Milwaukee, at which the Eastern and Western Reform rabbis made peace and designated the Emanu-El Seminary in New York to serve as a preparatory school for the Hebrew Union College. With that agreement having been made, Morais must surely have realized that the Reform-dominated Union would certainly never endorse a proposal for a competing rabbinical school in Philadelphia; and it was only a matter of time before he came to the realization that, in order to fulfill his dream of training traditional American rabbis, a new seminary was necessary.

---

[41]Letter from Jacob Ezekiel to Morais, March 8, 1877, Morais Papers.
[42]Letter from Jacob Ezekiel to Morais, Sept. 30, 1878, Morais Papers.

CHAPTER II

The Road to the Seminary

T he decade of the 1880's opened with great hope for the growing American Jewish community. Long past were the Wise-Leeser controversies, the fiery, strife-torn rabbinical conferences. Instead, it seemed to many observers that a new era was dawning for American Judaism, an age of peace and tranquillity, of mutual respect and admiration, in which Reform and Orthodoxy would learn to live and work together in harmony and in cooperation. In December, 1880, the *American Hebrew* declared,

> The era of fraternity and good will between the metropolitan congregations is a new one, and is the happy result of many decades of animosity, open and concealed, which marked the intercourse between Synagogue with Temple [sic], and Synagogue with Synagogue . . . They were times of keen feeling and heated controversy. The wave of Reform struck the rock of Orthodoxy, and in the hissing breakers and foaming rage many a good vessel of religion was sorely shaken, many a hoarse cry or hateful taunt was heard. But now the feelings are less excited, the struggle less violent, each party sees its errors, as well as those of its opponents, and the near future will doubtless bring about a unification and harmonization of views.[1]

A year later, the *American Hebrew* was even more glowing:

> The battles have been fought and the blessings of peace have been realized. Orthodoxy has seen Reform come to stay; it confronts it today as an established, unmistakable fact. Reform has seen, or at least [is] beginning to suspect that a halt must be cried somewhere and now that it has somewhat discarded the habitual sneer at Orthodoxy, it

---

[1]*AH*, Dec. 10, 1880, p. 38.

commences to appreciate the stability and comfort which the old faith, with all its imperfections, afforded.[2]

That such a wholly inaccurate portrait of American Jewry could be presented by a major periodical at the beginning of the decade which witnessed the Treyfa Banquet, the Pittsburgh Conference, and the founding of the Seminary can be attributed not only to wishful thinking, but also to the false sense of harmony engendered by the growth of such "non-denominational" institutions as the New York Board of Jewish Ministers and the Hebrew Union College. If Reform and Orthodoxy appeared less strident and more respectful in their approach towards one another, if they could co-operate in benevolent and even educational enterprises, surely a new era was dawning in which, perhaps, a true American *minhag* could be worked out, and a real sense of unity could be achieved. Nevertheless, within the short span of less than a decade, all of these dreams would be shattered, and the hopes for unity would be irrevocably lost. As we study the events and the causes which led to the foundation of the Seminary, we shall see that the *American Hebrew*'s optimistic portrait of American Judaism in the early 1880's was, indeed, an illusion, and that, given the nature of the personalities and the ideologies involved, the rifts that developed were truly inevitable.

The primary cause for the founding of the Seminary in 1886 was the disillusionment and, later, hostility that the traditionalists felt towards Isaac Mayer Wise and the Hebrew Union College, a disillusionment that began even before the Treyfa banquet of 1883 and the Pittsburgh Conference of 1885. To an extraordinary degree, the opposition to Wise and, by extension, to his college was personal in nature. Outspoken and overbearing, in the words of Rebekah Kohut, "Rabbi Wise seemed to have a genius for creating enmity."[3] Perhaps the harshest criticism of Wise is found not in the words of an opponent, but rather in those of a supporter, David Philipson, a member of the first graduating class of the Hebrew Union College.

---

[2]Ibid., January 13, 1882, p. 2.

[3]Rebekah Kohut, *As I Know Them, Some Jews and A Few Gentiles* (Garden City, N.Y., 1939), p. 206.

In his published writings, Philipson took every opportunity to extol Wise as the greatest leader of American Judaism; but in his personal, unpublished diary, Philipson's words took on a totally different character. Writing of Wise in his diary in September, 1890, Philipson confided,

> he is a man of great, of vast learning, of mighty energy but of a very envious and jealous disposition. He cannot endure that anyone shall stand near him, independent in thought and in action; he must rule; the name the Jewish Pope has been well applied to him ... When in time the true verdict will have been passed upon Dr. W. it will read in this wise: a man who did much for Judaism but who made everything subserve his own ambition; he would use every means to crush his opponents.[4]

Although much of the criticism of Wise stemmed from the standard Reform-Traditionalist controversy, the fact that he was president of the supposedly "non-denominational" Hebrew Union College proved especially grating to the traditionalists and eventually turned them against the College itself. As early as 1881, the *American Hebrew* attacked Wise for proclaiming that all Jewish law, except for the Ten Commandments, can be changed: "He who denies the authenticity of the Pentateuch is, in the minds of many, unfitted for the position of a Jewish teacher. He who holds that Mosaic legislation is no longer binding should, according to others, be debarred from the place of Rabbi." Epitomizing the traditionalists' attitude towards the rise of Reform, the newspaper continued, "The very foundations of Judaism are endangered. The rights of the Rabbis must be defined and limited!"[5]

A year later, the *American Hebrew* openly castigated the College itself for the Reform views of one of its faculty members, attacking Adolf Moses, an H.U.C. professor known for his anti-traditional outlook. The editors called upon Wise "to free the institution from such

---

[4]Stanley F. Chyet, "Isaac Mayer Wise: Portraits by David Philipson," in *A Bicentennial Festschrift for Jacob Rader Marcus*, Bertram W. Korn, ed. (N.Y., 1976) p. 87.

[5]*AH*, Jan. 28, 1881, p. 122.

a bigoted and partisan position";[6] and, two weeks later they again attacked Dr. Moses's Reform views as "contrary to the name and character of the College, which is not alone 'Hebrew' but a *Hebrew Union* College."[7]

Although Wise repeatedly defended the "non-denominational" character of the Hebrew Union College, any remaining illusions of the traditionalists were shattered by the controversy surrounding the so-called "Treyfa Banquet" of July 1883. The facts of the case are very simple, although their interpretation has been debated for the past one hundred years. On Wednesday, July 11, 1883, the Hebrew Union College held its first rabbinical graduation. Four young men—Israel Aaron, Henry Berkowitz, Joseph Krauskopf, and David Philipson—all of whom were to go on to distinguished careers in the Reform rabbinate, were ordained as rabbis by Isaac Mayer Wise and the faculty of the College. It was a glorious day in the history of American Judaism, the first rabbinical ordination ever held in the United States; and distinguished rabbis such as Benjamin Szold, Gustav Gottheil, and Kaufmann Kohler, had come from all over the country to participate in the ceremonies. At 7:30 in the evening, a gala banquet was held in the Highland House, a well-known Cincinnati catering establishment, and all of the guests, both Traditional and Reform, were invited to attend. Nevertheless, to the dismay of the traditionalists, who stormed out in protest, the menu included little neck clams, soft-shell crabs, shrimp, and frogs' legs, plus beef and ice cream and cheese.[8]

To this day, the debate rages as to who was responsible for the menu of the banquet, which appeared to be a deliberate insult and slap at the sensibilities of the traditionalists. Isaac Mayer Wise repeatedly ascribed the incident to the error of an "unscrupulous caterer";[9] and his denial of any responsibility for the affair seems reasonable, for as Michael A. Meyer asserts, "it was politically so preposterous a *faux pas* that he would never have allowed it to happen."[10] Nevertheless, to assume that such a menu could have

---

[6]Ibid., August 18, 1882, p. 2.

[7]Ibid., Sept. 1, 1882, p. 26.

[8] John J. Appel, "The Treyfa Banquet," in *Commentary*, Feb . 1966, p . 75 .

[9]*American Israelite*, August 3, 1884, p 4.

[10]Meyer, "Centennial History," p. 41.

been presented merely by accident taxes the imagination; and John Appel therefore asserts that "the treyfa banquet was deliberately arranged, probably without Wise's knowledge, by some of his supporters among Cincinnati businessmen."[11] According to Appel, "the Highland House dinner is a nearly perfect expression of the assimilationist tendencies among American Jews in the 19th century, especially among German Jews. So strong was the propensity of the members of the Banquet Committee to regard conformity to gentile norms as an unquestioned virtue, that they deliberately chose to make an issue of serving *treyfa* food in public."[12]

As one might imagine, the Treyfa Banquet provoked a storm of protest from the traditionalist forces in American Judaism, who interpreted it as a direct slap at their honor and their beliefs, and who refused to listen to any of Wise's explanations. In the words of the *American Hebrew*, the banquet was "a systematic and public insult to Jewish law,"[13] and the newspaper facetiously asked, "Does the eleventh chapter of Leviticus form any part of the college edition of the Pentateuch?"[14] Indeed, almost the entire American Jewish press, including the *Jewish Messenger*, *Jewish Record*, *Hebrew Standard*, and *Jewish Tribune*, roundly condemned the forces who organized the banquet. Even many a Reformer probably echoed the words of the *Jewish Tribune*:

> It was an unmitigated disgrace . . . though we ourselves do open and above board disregard such dietary laws, be they biblical or rabbinical, which are absolutely obsolete, we are liberal enough to respect the honest feelings of those who differ from us.[15]

Although there is a tendency today among Jewish historians to downplay the impact of the Treyfa Banquet as a cause for the founding of the Seminary and to stress the inevitability of the rift that produced the institution,[16] the truth of the matter is that it was

---

[11]Appel, p. 76.
[12]Ibid., pp. 77-78.
[13]*AH*, July 20, 1883, p. 110.
[14]Ibid., July 27, 1883, cover page.
[15]Quoted in *AH*, July 27, 1883, p. 127.
[16]Meyer, "Centennial History," p. 41.

not the banquet itself that provoked the ire of the traditionalists, but rather the almost maniacal reaction of Isaac Mayer Wise to their complaints. Instead of merely stressing the fact that the banquet occurred through the error of the caterer—as he most probably believed—and that it was given by private individuals, Wise again and again in the pages of the *American Israelite* railed against "kitchen Judaism" and the Jewish dietary laws, asserting, "It is about time to stop that noise over the culinary department of Judaism. The American Hebrew's religion centers not in kitchen and stomach. The *American Israelite* begs to be excused, it does not deal in victuals. It has some more important matters to attend to."[17] It was Wise's repeated assertions that the dietary laws had lost their validity and the sneering contempt that he displayed towards the orthodox that provoked the ire of the traditionalists and prompted them to consider founding another institution for the training of American rabbis.

In Philadelphia, the *Jewish Record* bitterly condemned Wise's attitude, asking,

> What does the head of the 'Union College' expect to achieve by the above tirade of abuse—this scoffing at the dietary laws held in reverence by many congregations now in the "Union." Is it a challenge for those who have not rejected Moses to follow Wise to sever their connections with the U.A.H.C. and withdraw their support from an institution, for the education of Jewish ministers, whose chief instructor openly reviles the Mosaic laws? It looks so. . .[18]

One could very well ask the question as to what were the motives of Isaac Mayer Wise in so severely alienating the traditionalists and belittling one of the pillars of Jewish observance. After all, up to this time, Wise had gone out of his way to keep up the appearance of non-denominationalism at the Hebrew Union College; and he had carefully cultivated the support and cooperation of traditionalists such as Sabato Morais, Benjamin Szold, and Marcus Jastrow. In the opinion of John Appel,

---

[17]*American Israelite*, August 3, 1884, p.4.
[18]*Jewish Record*, August 10, 1883.

A study of the *'treyfa* banquet' inevitably leads to a somewhat altered portrait of Rabbi Wise, who has hitherto been considered as a *moderate* Reformer. At least in this affair, he fought back stubbornly, tactlessly, and with a zeal seemingly out of all proportion to the cause at issue. His editorials reveal a man apparently neither caring for nor understanding the deep hold of traditional practice on his fellow Jews.[19]

Nevertheless, Wise was a consummate politician, and whether he was genuinely moderate or not, he must have had some definite reason for distancing himself so greatly from the traditionalists at that time. One possible explanation is that he longed to turn the Hebrew Union College into a decidedly Reform institution without any of the trappings or hindrances imposed by pretending to serve all aspects of the American Jewish community. It is also possible that, since he felt that most American Jews no longer observed the dietary laws, he hoped to turn the banquet into a *cause celebre*, in which there would be a ground swell of support for Reform ideals, thereby discrediting the traditionalist leaders, even in their own congregations.

Whatever his motivations, Isaac Mayer Wise's plan surely backfired, for in the two years between the Treyfa Banquet and the Pittsburgh Conference, the traditionalists began to lay the foundations for a new Seminary. The Union of American Hebrew Congregations, the parent body of the College, was thoroughly discredited in the eyes of men such as Frederick de Sola Mendes, Benjamin Szold, and Marcus Jastrow, all of whom tried to induce their synagogues to leave the organization.[20] The attitude of the traditionalists is mirrored in the pages of their unofficial organ, the *American Hebrew*, which, starting in January, 1884, in the wake of the controversy over the Treyfa Banquet, launched a series of editorials aimed at demolishing support for Wise and for his College:

> For a Hebrew Union College as an institution we have but admiration; it is a nucleus that can expand and become a powerful factor in conscientious Judaism. But against Wise as President of the College that is to

---

[19]Appel, p. 78.
[20]Mendes and Jastrow were both successful in this endeavor.

represent Judaism and rear the teachers of the next generation, and against that College which has as its President a man who sneers at the Mosaic food-laws and their latter-day endorsement by science, and who next declares that no laws exist against intermarriage with non-Jews; against a College which has as its Professor of Homiletics(!) a man who would enshrine Christmas in the Jewish calendar, we have much, very much to object. Such men have no right to teach ministers who shall claim to be Jewish, for such doctrines are anti-Jewish, and a College which retains the service of such men is simply not a Jewish College, and is not entitled to appeal to Jews for its support to the amount of one dollar.[21]

Six weeks later, the newspaper once again condemned "the unbalanced conduct" of Isaac Mayer Wise, and called for his removal from the office of President of the College. Realizing the futility of their demand, the editors proposed an "alternative": "to have another college, to begin all over again . . . The work can begin at once, its scale is small, its expenses slight. It will need no costly building, it will need no pompous 'reports' to be printed and circulated to keep up public spirit."[22] By April, the editors had become downright threatening in referring to Wise: "we will promise him only that he shall hear from us when we are ready to draw the curtain, and he shall awaken to find that he is not 'president of the only Jewish College in America!'"[23]

In Philadelphia, the *Jewish Record*, which was very similar to the *American Hebrew* in its outlook, also began to call for the establishment of another rabbinical college in the East. On February 1, 1884, an individual identified only as "J.W." sent a letter to the editor of the *Record*, asserting that, "Fully three fourths of the congregations of the East would not receive men holding the opinions which graduates of the Cincinnati College would and do hold. Their course is therefore plain. They must withdraw from the college and establish another."[24] The following week, Rev. F. de Sola Mendes

---

[21]*AH*, January 4, 1884, cover page.
[22]Ibid., Feb. 15, 1884, p. 2.
[23]Ibid., April 18, 1884, p. 2.
[24]*Jewish Record*, Feb. 1, 1884, n.p.

also wrote in to call for the establishment of a new college;[25] and, by
the end of the month, the paper itself demanded the removal of
Isaac Mayer Wise from his position as head of H.U.C.[26] As the year
rolled on, the *Jewish Record* warmly embraced the concept of a new
institution, and it issued a challenge: "Who will come forward and
initiate the good work?"[27]

The two rabbis who took the strongest stand against Isaac
Mayer Wise and the Hebrew Union College were Marcus Jastrow
and Sabato Morais, both of Philadelphia. Whereas Jastrow sought to
protest and effect change through the medium of the Union of
American Hebrew Congregations, as well as from the pulpit,
Morais, whose synagogue never joined the Union, did not hesitate
to endorse a drastic solution to the problems of the College. In a
Chanukah sermon delivered in December, 1884, Morais declared,

> To save the religion for which Mattathias staked his existence and of
> which Chanukah is a glorious exponent, a seminary of learning, where
> *all* the ordinances of the Pentateuch, compatible with our state of dis-
> persion, will be taught and enforced, must be set up in in obedience to
> the demands of an enlightened 'Orthodoxy.'[28]

From that point on, week after week, whether from the pulpit, or in
the pages of the *American Hebrew* or the *Jewish Record*, Morais repeatedly called for the establishment of a new seminary. Thus, well
before the Pittsburgh Conference of November 16-18, 1885, the
foundations of the new institution were being laid by the traditionalists.

Looking back from the perspective of one hundred years later,
the "platform" which was formulated by nineteen Reform rabbis at
Pittsburgh appears to be merely a comprehensive summary of the
theological position of Reform in the latter half of the nineteenth
century. Although the conference was chaired by Isaac Mayer Wise,
the platform, which consisted of eight articles or "planks," was

---

[25]Ibid., Feb. 8, 1884, n.p.
[26]Ibid., Feb. 29, 1884, n.p.
[27]Ibid., Dec. 5, 1884, n.p.
[28]*AH*, Dec. 19, 1884, p. 84.

principally the work of Kaufmann Kohler.[29] In its denial of ceremonial law, Kashruth, the Messiah, and the return to Eretz Yisrael, the platform certainly offered nothing new; and, indeed, in its first reaction to the document, the *American Hebrew* virtually congratulated the Reform rabbis who assembled at Pittsburgh for their moderation:

> Inasmuch as six of the eight resolutions adopted at the Pittsburg Conference of Reform Rabbis are accepted as conservative doctrine, they form a wise and temperate platform, remarkable mainly for two facts, which we have frequently emphasized—first, that the chief differences between so-called Orthodoxy and so-called Reform are mainly differences in words; and secondly that the principles of Judaism, whether expounded by Conservative or Reform teachers, are such as to attract the thoughtful despite the great religious resolutions of the past century.[30]

According to the *American Hebrew*, the only non-traditional "planks" enacted at Pittsburgh were the denial of Kashruth and the restoration to Palestine; and the editors concluded, "Taken in all, the platform is a far more conservative one than we had hoped for . . . American Judaism can easily be united."

Nevertheless, within a week, the entire American Jewish community exploded in an uproar and a violent debate over the results of the conference; and the *American Hebrew* did a complete about-face in its appraisal of the Platform, condemning Wise for participating in a "Rabbinical conference which avowedly professes to create a sectarian Jewish party."[31] While it is certainly possible that the editors changed their minds about the implications of the Pittsburgh Platform, it is just as probable that the newspaper and the traditionalists who supported it consciously chose to make an issue out of the results of the conference, in order to stir up support for their

---

[29]Moshe Davis, "Jewish Religious Life and Institutions in America (A Historical Study)," in *The Jews: Their Religion and Culture*, ed. Louis Finkelstein (N.Y., 1971), Vol. 2, p. 307; For the full text of the platform, see Davis, *Emergence*, pp. 226-227.

[30]*AH*, Nov. 20, 1885, p. 27.

[31]Ibid. Nov. 27, 1885, cover page.

projected seminary. Sabato Morais, for example, delivered a fiery discourse denouncing the Pittsburgh rabbis and the Hebrew Union College; and he concluded with a call for Shearith Israel in New York, America's premier traditional congregation, to establish "a seminary of learning devoted to cultured Orthodoxy."[32]

Another Philadelphia Jewish leader, Dr. Solomon Solis Cohen, also attacked the results of the conference as "a step backward"; and he was particularly offended by the Platform's apparent denial of revelation and of the return to Palestine, as well as by what he considered to be the rejection of the concept of a personal Deity.[33] In Philadelphia, the *Jewish Record* labelled the Pittsburgh Conference, "sound and fury, signifying nothing"; and it asserted that, "to maintain the integrity of Judaism there is no other course left but complete severance from the Cincinnati College and the establishment of a university devoted to the interests of conservative Judaism."[34]

For his part, Isaac Mayer Wise staunchly defended the results of the conclave, vigorously condemning "those semi, demi, three-fourths and self-constituted orthodox gentlemen and judges of their brethren who have so much to say against the Pittsburg Conference."[35] Week after week, he published the full Platform in the pages of the *American Israelite*, calling it a "declaration of independence" for American Judaism. Wise's principal contention was that the traditional patterns of Jewish belief and observance had lost all meaning for modern American Jews; and therefore the Platform's ideas would eventually become normative Judaism for the United States. Proudly he asserted, "We Are the orthodox Jews in America, and they WERE the orthodoxy of former days and other countries."[36] Addressing the traditionalists, he declared, "You do not represent the ideas and sentiments of the American Jews . . . you are an anachronism, strangers in this country and to your brethren. You represent yourselves, together with a past age and a foreign land."[37]

---

[32]Ibid., Nov. 27, 1885, p. 5.

[33]Ibid., Nov. 27, 1885, pp. 40-41.

[34]*Jewish Record*, Nov. 27, 1885, n.p.

[35]*American Israelite*, Dec. 18, 1885, p. 6.

[36]Ibid.. Nov. 27, 1885, p.4.

[37]Ibid., Nov. 27, 1885, p. 4; See also, Dec. 4, 1885, p. 6.

Nevertheless, stung by the criticism of moderate leaders like Benjamin Szold, and threatened with the possibility of defections from the U.A.H.C., Wise backed off somewhat from his belligerent stand. He pointed out that there were over 100 congregations in the Union, while the Pittsburgh Conference represented the opinions of less than 20% of their rabbis; and therefore the Platform could in no way be considered binding for the entire U.A.H.C. Responding to a query from Congregation Ahavath Chesed of New York, Alexander Kohut's synagogue, which wrote to find out if the doctrines expressed at Pittsburgh were the official policy of the Hebrew Union College, Wise declared, *"The enactments, resolutions, or proceedings of the Pittsburg Rabbinical Conference, or of any other Conference, except the Council of the Union of American Hebrew Congregations have nothing in the world to do with the course of studies or the methods of teaching adopted in the Hebrew Union College."*[38] Although Wise may have hoped to keep many "middle-of-the-road" congregations within the fold of the Union and loyal to the College by denying any official status to the Pittsburgh Platform, both with regard to the U.A.H.C. and to the Hebrew Union College, his words could not prevent the inevitable, for within a few weeks of the conference, concrete plans were formalized for the foundation of the Jewish Theological Seminary.

Before we begin a discussion of the actual founding of the Seminary, we would do well to take a closer look at some of the leading figures involved in the creation of the institution. The man who did more than anyone else to make the Seminary a reality was, without a doubt, the Reverend Sabato Morais of Congregation Mikveh Israel of Philadelphia.[39] Born in Leghorn (Livorno), Italy, on April 13, 1823, Morais was descended from Portuguese Marranos on his father's side, and from German Ashkenazim on his mother's side. He received a thorough Jewish education from the rabbis of his local community, and in August, 1845, Rabbi Avraham Baruch

---

[38]Ibid., Dec. 18, 1885, p. 6.
[39]For a biography of Morais, See Davis, *Emergence*, p. 354.

Piperno of Leghorn awarded him a *semicha* certificate, enabling him to teach and to serve as a *hazzan* in the Sephardic community, but without the more advanced title of *Hacham*. Morais also received a comprehensive secular education; and he was well acquainted with Italian, Spanish, and French literature. His father, Samuel, was a passionate supporter of Italian independence; and, as a young man, Sabato came to share his father's principles, becoming close friends with the great Italian patriot, Joseph Mazzini.

In 1845, Morais tried unsuccessfully to gain the position of Assistant *Hazzan* at the Spanish and Portuguese Synagogue of London, Sha'ar Ha-Shamayim, but the following year he returned to London to serve as the "Master of Hebrew" in the Orphans' School run by the synagogue. In addition, in London, Morais served as the private tutor to several aristocratic Anglo-Jewish families, most notably the Montefiores; and it is interesting to note that, a generation later, Solomon Schechter, Morais's successor at the Seminary, served as a private tutor to Claude Montefiore before coming to America. Meanwhile, in the United States, the Rev. Isaac Leeser had a quarrel with the Board of Congregation Mikveh Israel in 1849, and subsequently resigned from his position as *hazzan* of that synagogue. Upon hearing of the vacancy in the congregation in Philadelphia, Morais came to America in 1851, preached at Mikveh Israel, and was elected as *hazzan* in April, thereby beginning his forty-six year association with that synagogue.

At Mikveh Israel, Morais distinguished himself not only for his exceptional cantorial skills, but also for his great ability as a speaker and as a writer; and, like Isaac Leeser, Morais made it his custom to preach every week. Remembering his republican heritage from Italy, during the Civil War Morais was an outspoken opponent of slavery and a fervent supporter of the Union cause; and, for a while, the board of his synagogue even tried to prevent him from speaking out on controversial issues.[40] Throughout his career, Morais was involved in causes that today would be termed "social action." For example, in 1890, he helped to mediate the Philadelphia

---

[40]Charles J. Cohen, "Dr. Morais's Relationship to the Congregation," in *Commemoration of the One Hundredth Anniversary of the Birth of the Reverend Doctor Sabato Morais* (Phila., 1924) p. 11.

Cloakmakers' Strike, along with Rabbis Marcus Jastrow and Joseph Krauskopf; and he also became a true champion of the rights of the Jewish immigrants from Eastern Europe.[41] Morais was also involved in supporting the early Jewish farming communities in Southern New Jersey, and helped interest Baron de Hirsch in this project.[42] In 1887, Morais was distinguished as the first Jew to receive an honorary LL.D. degree from the University of Pennsylvania.

Although he was not a critical scholar in the modern sense, Morais was an extraordinarily learned and erudite rabbi and an expert in Hebrew literature, a language which he wrote most beautifully. In 1887, celebrating his award from the University of Pennsylvania, the *American Hebrew* proclaimed, "He is the greatest master of Hebrew composition and in many respects, the most accomplished Hebraist in America."[43] Morais saw himself as a spiritual disciple of the great Italian Jewish scholar, Samuel David Luzzatto, and he translated and published several of Luzzatto's works for the American public, along with various studies of different facets of Italian Jewish literature. Although at first Morais opposed the foundation of the Jewish Publication Society, since it was led by the Reform Rabbi Joseph Krauskopf, he eventually came to serve on the Consultation Committee for the Society's Bible project, and translated the Book of Jeremiah for the J.P.S. edition of *The Holy Scriptures*. As a teacher of Judaism, Morais excelled; and, over the years, he created a highly devoted group of private adult students, such as Solomon Solis Cohen, Cyrus Adler, and Isaac Husik. Years after leaving Philadelphia, for example, Cyrus Adler would write to Morais asking his opinion of the latest critical and philological interpretations of the Bible.[44]

In terms of his theology, Morais was the principal exponent of what was called in his day "enlightened Orthodoxy," an outlook which would be somewhere between the standpoints of present-day Conservative and Modern Orthodox Judaism. In the words of his son, Henry, "To the radical he was ultra-Orthodox, as the most pro-

[41]Whiteman, "Leeser," p. 56.
[42]*Proceedings*, J.T.S.A., 1898. p. 85.
[43]*AH*, June 17, 1887, p. 2.
[44]See letter from Cyrus Adler to S. Morais, Oct. 23, 1884, Morais Papers.

nounced of that type could possibly be; to the ultra-Orthodox, the overdoing pietist, the bigot, he was not Orthodox."[45] When dealing with questions of synagogue ritual, for example, Morais strongly upheld the traditional practices: he vigorously opposed late Friday evening services, the playing of an organ, and mixed seating, and took a dim view of any rabbi who would unilaterally seek to change the traditional *siddur* or substitute English for Hebrew.[46] Nevertheless, Morais did not feel that all the laws and customs included in the *Shulchan Aruch* were immutable; and he declared that if a synod of traditional and responsible American rabbis were assembled, they would have the authority to make great changes in the synagogue service. Writing in the *Jewish Messenger* in 1875, Morais outlined a proposal for a shortened and modernized service which would suit the temperament of American Jews:

A judicious selection from our Psalter, interspersed with the best Hebrew hymns from ancient and modern poets, the rehearsing of the benedictions, preceding and succeeding the 'Shemang' [sic] which, beyond all doubt, date from a period of remote antiquity; the 'Shemone Esre,' so-called or Amidah, the perusal of the Law in triennial cycle, if it is universally adopted by the Hebrew Community in the United States, and becomes thereby a settled custom, as it was with Palestinian Jews . . . together with a rightly chosen chapter from the prophetic writings might be the formulary for each morning of Sabbath and festivals.[47]

Another area in which Morais differed from the traditional point of view was that of the restoration of the sacrifices in the Messianic era. Although Morais would not dare to say that the sacrifices should be abolished nor that people should cease to pray for them, he asserted that prayer was definitely more important than sacrifices, and that God Himself might abolish the sacrifices in the

---

[45]Henry Morais, "Memoir," in *Proceedings*, J.T.S.A., 1898, p. 79.
[46]See letter from S. Morais to Frederick de Sola Mendes, May 13, 1888, in Morais Papers.
[47]*Jewish Messenger*, Dec. 10, 1875 p. 5.

world-to-come.[48] Living in an age in which Bible scholars seemed to take a savage delight in carving up Scripture, Morais flatly refused to condone any "higher" or source criticism for the books of the Torah. Nevertheless, when it came to the other books of the Bible—the Prophets and Writings—his views were not so strict. Thus, in a sermon on the Book of Jonah, delivered in 1897, he declared, "Notwithstanding the care of our copyists to avoid errors, it may have happened that discrepancies about names, dates, localities or even narrative of some events may have crept in.[49]

Although from his earliest childhood Morais followed the Sephardic *minhag*, when it came to religious practice he often stated that he felt that the various *minhagim*—Russian, Polish, German, Italian, Sephardic, etc.—were merely accidents of history; and he longed for the day when these differences would be abolished, particularly in the United States, where their retention was pointless. In his personal life, despite his feelings that Jewish law could be changed by the consent of competent authorities, Morais remained a fully observant Jew in the traditional sense; and he was especially punctilious with regard to the observance of the Sabbath.[50]

As his chief co-worker in the founding of the Seminary, Morais chose the Reverend Henry Pereira Mendes, minister of the venerable Congregation Shearith Israel in New York City.[51] Born in Birmingham, England, on April 13, 1852, Pereira Mendes (he never used the name Henry) was the son of Rev. Abraham Pereira Mendes, who later served as rabbi in Newport, Rhode Island, and was the younger brother of Rev. Frederick de Sola Mendes, who served for over forty years in the pulpit of Congregation Shaaray Tefilah in Manhattan. As a youngster, Pereira Mendes attended Northwick College, an English Hebrew day school that had been founded by his father. Upon completing high school, Mendes went on to the University College of London, where he received a Master

---

[48]See S. Morais, sermon, "Is the Sacrificial Rite or Prayer the Most Acceptable Service," n.d., in Morais Papers.

[49]S. Morais, "Sermon on Jonah," 1897, Morais Papers.

[50]See Max Samuel Nussenbaum, *Champion of Orthodox Judaism: A Biography of the Reverend Sabato Morais, LL.D.*, D.H.L. Dissertation, Bernard Revel Graduate School, Yeshiva University, 1964.

[51]For a biography of Mendes, see Davis, *Emergence*, p. 351.

of Arts degree, and then decided to embark upon a rabbinical career.

Although he received an adequate elementary Jewish education from his father and other tutors, the extent of Mendes's Jewish knowledge is uncertain. As Eugene Markovitz notes,

> It is doubtful if he received *Semicha* in the traditional manner, or if he mastered the required knowledge of *Yoreh Deah*, Talmud, and Codes. There is little to indicate in his subsequent sermons or writings that he excelled in these particular fields. There is no question, however, that the Chief Rabbinate in England, as well as the Sephardic Rabbi of the Bevis Marks Synagogue, fully accepted him as a rabbi and minister.[52]

From 1874 to 1877, Mendes served as minister to the Sephardic congregation in Manchester, England, and then, through the good efforts of his older brother, Frederick, he came to New York in the summer of 1877 to serve as the assistant *hazzan* to the Rev. J.J. Lyons at the prestigious Congregation Shearith Israel. When Lyons passed away the following month, Mendes succeeded him as senior minister to the congregation, a position that he held until his retirement in 1920.

Like Sabato Morais in Philadelphia, Pereira Mendes was involved in almost every area of Jewish community endeavor in New York City, and like Morais, his relationship with his congregation was often a stormy one.[53] For many years, Mendes was involved in combatting a movement for reforms in his synagogue; and in 1884, he actually received an M.D. degree from New York University in preparation for leaving the rabbinate. In addition to his work on behalf of the Seminary, Mendes helped to found the New York Board of Jewish Ministers, the Union of Orthodox Jewish Congregations, and the Federation of American Zionists, serving as an officer of each organization. Mendes took a vigorous role in aiding impoverished or oppressed Jews around the world, particularly in Morocco, Russia, and Palestine, and he served as the first president of the New York Chapter of the Alliance Israelite Universelle.

---

[52]Eugene Markovitz, *Henry Pereira Mendes (1877-1920)*, D.H.L. Dissertation, Bernard Revel Graduate School, Yeshiva University, 1961, p. 7.
[53]Ibid., p. 16.

Realizing the tremendous need for improved Jewish education, Mendes wrote many works for Jewish youngsters; and he also took an active role in helping to provide Jewish education for the immigrants from Eastern Europe. Although Mendes's religious outlook, lifestyle, and Sephardic upbringing were very different from those of the Russian immigrants, they regarded him as a true friend and as the recognized spokesman for orthodox Judaism in New York. Thus, when "Chief Rabbi" Jacob Joseph came to New York in 1888 to serve as the spiritual head of a federation of Lower East Side congregations, the immigrants regarded it as a special sign of recognition that Mendes, along with Judge Philip J. Joachimsen, soon invited him to tour the Hebrew Orphan Asylum.[54]

With regard to his religious outlook, Mendes's views were very similar to those of Sabato Morais; and, like Morais, he saw himself as a defender of "enlightened Orthodoxy." He was one of the first orthodox leaders to stress the importance of adult education; and all of his published works are written on a popular level. Unusual for his day, Mendes was a strong believer in the value of interfaith activities, and he even invited a Protestant bishop to address his sisterhood, an action which would have been unthinkable for an Eastern European orthodox rabbi. In reaching out to Pereira Mendes for help in founding the Seminary, Sabato Morais was enlisting not only the leader of America's most prestigious traditional synagogue, but also a powerful orator and indefatigable worker who, hopefully, could rally the forces of New York Jewry to support the new institution.

Along with Pereira Mendes, Sabato Morais also gained the support of Alexander Kohut, the brilliant and dynamic rabbi of Congregation Ahavath Chesed of New York.[55] Kohut was born in Felegyhaza, Hungary, on April 22, 1842, to a family that was so poor that they could not even afford to send him to school until the age of nine. Completing his elementary studies in record time, Kohut continued his Jewish education in Budapest, and then went on to attend the Jewish Theological Seminary of Breslau where he studied with

---

[54]Abraham J. Karp, "New York Chooses a Chief Rabbi," in A.J. Karp, ed., *The Jewish Experience in America*, (N.Y./Waltham, 1969), Vol. 4, p. 157.

[55]For a biography of Kohut, see Davis, *Emergence*, p. 344.

Zacharias Frankel, Heinrich Graetz, and Jacob Bernays. Although the course of study in Breslau was seven years, Kohut completed his work in only five and one-half years, receiving his *semicha* from Frankel in 1867. Kohut was equally brilliant in secular studies. As a young man, he had mastered Arabic, Turkish, and Persian; and, while at Breslau, he also managed to study Semitics at the University of Leipzig, where he took a special interest in Persian studies. After his ordination by the Breslau Seminary, Kohut held several rabbinical positions in his native Hungary; and he also had the distinction of being the first Jew to serve as a regional public school supervisor in that country.[56] In addition, Kohut was chosen to serve as the Jewish representative to the Hungarian Parliament, but his departure for America in 1885 prevented him from taking his seat.

By the time that he arrived in the United States, Alexander Kohut had already earned a reputation as a first-rate Jewish critical scholar and author. At the age of twenty-one, he had published his first article, in Hungarian, on "The Social and Political Relations of the Jews In Rome"; and, while at Breslau, at the urging of Zacharias Frankel, he had "composed a thesis on the Parsic origin of the Jewish superstitious doctrines concerning angels and demons," for which the Universities of Breslau and Leipzig jointly awarded him a doctorate *honoris causa.*[57] In 1867, at the request of the Hungarian Academy of Sciences, to which he was later elected, Kohut wrote on "The Talmud and Parseeism"; and he later wrote detailed articles on the Book of Tobit, Second Isaiah, and Persian mythology. In 1878, Kohut published the first volume of his *magnum opus*, the *Aruch Completum*, an enormous Talmudic dictionary which took twenty-four years to complete, and which was not finished until four years after he came to America. In the United States, Kohut continued his scholarly writing, not only completing the *Aruch*, but also publishing a commentary on *Pirke Avot*, and writing many articles, such as

---

[56]Moshe Davis, *Yahadut Amerika Be-hitpathutah (Toldot Haascola Hahistorit Bimaya Hatsha-esray)* (N.Y., 1951), p. 76.

[57]George Alexander Kohut, "A Memoir of Dr. Alexander Kohut's Literary Activity," in *Proceedings*, J.T.S.A., 1894, p. 3.

"The Zendavesta and the First Eleven Chapters of Genesis," which appeared in the *Jewish Quarterly Review* in 1890.[58]

While it would seem unlikely for a scholar of such credentials to have come to America in the 1880's, Kohut's reason for doing so was purely personal, not professional, in nature. His first wife, Julia, had developed an extremely serious illness in Hungary; and when her personal physician moved to the United States, the Kohut family followed in a vain attempt to save her life.[59] Thus it came about that when the pulpit of Congregation Ahavath Chesed of New York City became vacant due to the death of its rabbi, Adolph Huebsch, Alexander Kohut successfully applied for the position, arriving in May, 1885. The synagogue was, at the time, a definitely Reform congregation. Not only did it have mixed seating, it also employed a drastically abridged and altered German and Hebrew prayerbook edited by Dr. Huebsch, it did not celebrate the festivals of Purim and Chanukah, nor the additional day of the other festivals mandated for the diaspora, and it shunned the traditional order of Torah readings. Upon his arrival, Kohut proceeded to give the synagogue a more traditional tone, introducing Chanukah and Purim and adopting the reading of the proper *sedrah* each week.[60] Nevertheless, Ahavath Chesed continued to use the Huebsch prayerbook, with a new English translation prepared by Dr. Kohut; and with its radical abridgement of the service and its elimination of such traditional concepts as the return to Zion and the Messiah, this *siddur* was far more extreme than any prayerbook that might be used in a Conservative synagogue today.[61]

On a theological level, Kohut saw himself as a defender of tradition and law against the antinomian tendencies of Reform Judaism. In the words of Bernard Drachman, "Dr. Kohut was a strong believer in the authority of Jewish tradition and the bindingness of rabbinic law," and his espousal of tradition, therefore,

---

[58]Ibid., p. 12.

[59]Rebekah Kohut, *My Portion* (N.Y., 1925), p. 91.

[60]Davis, *Yahadut Amerika*, p. 80.

[61]See Alexander Kohut trans., *Prayers for the Divine Services of Congregation Ahawath Chesed*, arranged by Dr. A. Huebsch (N.Y., 1889).

"produced a tremendous furore in the ranks of Reform Jewry."[62] While Kohut admitted the possibility of changes in Judaism, he felt that tradition was the anchor that modern Jews needed to maintain their ancestral faith in nineteenth-century America.

In June, 1885, Dr. Kohut delivered an impassioned Shavuot sermon on *Pirke Avot*, stressing the chain of Jewish tradition from Moses down to the present. The following week, the distinguished Reform Rabbi Kaufmann Kohler of Temple Beth El countered with a sermon entitled "Are we Progressing or Retrograding," in which he attempted to refute Kohut's arguments by asserting that "Mosaic Rabbinical Judaism is retrospective," looking only to the past, while Reform is concerned with the Jewish future.[63] Thus, the great rabbinical debate, known as the Kohut-Kohler controversy, was begun; and it raged throughout the summer of 1885 in the press and in the pulpit. Kohut published his sallies in the pages of the *American Hebrew*, where he was supported by such worthies as Sabato Morais and Pereira Mendes; whereas Kohler published his arguments in the *New York Herald*, winning the support of Rabbi Gustav Gottheil of the prestigious Temple Emanu-El.[64] The great debate attracted the attention of Jews all across the United States; and years later, Kohut's second wife, Rebekah, would relate how she and her father, Rabbi Albert S. Bettelheim, living in far-away San Francisco, would avidly wait for the arrival of the Jewish newspapers so as to follow the latest developments in the controversy.[65] Kohut's eloquent arguments in the debate established him as a distinguished national spokesman for the Jewish tradition; and along with his impeccable scholarly credentials, his newly-acquired prestige made him an important ally for Morais in the founding of the Seminary. In addition, there was a natural rivalry between the Jewish communities of the East and West, and thus, by enlisting the aid of Kohut, Morais may have been attempting to woo those Eastern moderate Reform elements who wished to shift the center of American Jewish intellectual life from Cincinnati to New York.

---

[62]Bernard Drachman, *The Unfailing Light: Memoirs of an American Rabbi* (N.Y., 1948), pp. 176-177.

[63]*AH*, June 12, 1885. pp. 2-3.

[64]Philip Cowen, *Memories of An American Jew* (N.Y., 1932), p. 406.

[65]Rebekah Kohut, *My Portion*, p. 83.

Working along with Morais, Mendes, and Kohut, was a larger group of influential American rabbis who, in varying degrees, lent their moral and financial support to the projected institution. Among the more prominent were Rabbi Marcus Jastrow of Philadelphia, Rabbi Benjamin Szold of Baltimore, Rev. A. P. Mendes of Newport, Rabbi Frederick de Sola Mendes of New York, Rabbi Henry Schneeberger of Baltimore, and Rabbi Bernard Drachman of Newark, and later, New York, of whom we shall have more to say later on. As Morais's colleague in Philadelphia, Jastrow had taught with him on the faculty of Maimonides College. A traditionalist who accepted moderate reforms, Jastrow had served as rabbi of Congregation Rodeph Shalom in Philadelphia since his arrival in America in 1866; and, like Morais, he saw his goal as stemming the spread of Reform in his congregation and in his community. A tremendously learned scholar, Jastrow's *Dictionary of the Targumim, The Talmud Babli and Yerushalmi, and the Midrashic Literature* is still in use by rabbinical students today. Benjamin Szold, like Jastrow, was also a very scholarly rabbi, whose most famous work was a Hebrew commentary on the Book of Job. Serving in the Reform congregation Oheb Shalom of Baltimore, Szold was perhaps the most left-wing of all the early Seminary supporters; but he disagreed violently with the Reformers on such issues as the retention of Hebrew in the service, the Sabbath, and the dietary laws. Henry W. Schneeberger, rabbi of Baltimore's Chizuk Amuno Congregation, stands out not only because he was passionately devoted to the Seminary and helped to raise funds for it, but also because he was "the very first American-born ordained rabbi," having received his *semicha* from Rabbi Israel Hildesheimer in Berlin in 1871.[66]

Along with his rabbinical colleagues, Morais also enlisted the aid of a number of influential laymen in founding the Seminary; and although we shall discuss the lay leaders of the Seminary later on, it is fitting at this point to mention the names of David M. Piza and Joseph Blumenthal, both leaders of Congregation Shearith Israel in New York, as well as Dr. Cyrus Adler and Dr. Solomon Solis Cohen, who had become students and close friends of Morais in

---

[66]Israel M. Goldman, "Henry W. Schneeberger: His Role in American Judaism," *AJHQ*, LVII, no. 2 (Dec., 1967), p. 153.

Philadelphia. With this network of lay and rabbinical allies and supporters in place, Sabato Morais set out to found the Seminary.

CHAPTER III

Founding the Seminary

A s we have seen, as early as December, 1884, Sabato Morais had called for the establishment of a traditional seminary to counteract the Reformist tendencies of Isaac Mayer Wise's Hebrew Union College. In the aftermath of the Pittsburgh Conference, Morais intensified his resolve to start a new rabbinical seminary. He wrote to Henry Pereira Mendes in New York, asking him and his congregation, Shearith Israel, to take the lead in the establishment of the new institution.[1] With its burgeoning, daily growing Jewish population, Morais realized that New York was the most logical location for the new seminary; and also, he must surely have remembered the lackluster support that the Philadelphia Jewish community had given to Maimonides College. For his part, Pereira Mendes gladly agreed to help Morais, and he soon sent an appeal to his congregants, asking for their support.[2] In December, 1885, Morais also wrote to Alexander Kohut in New York, formally requesting his support for the Seminary project; and an active correspondence between the two men ensued, concerning the aims and methods of the institution.[3] In addition, Morais contacted influential lay leaders in both New York and Philadelphia, seeking their aid. Some years later, he would note that the Seminary initially took shape when "a few honest-hearted Jews . . . first met at my house to take counsel together."[4]

In New York, Morais's primary lay ally was David M. Piza, a wealthy Sephardic member of the board of Shearith Israel, who had

---

[1]*Jewish Record*, Dec. 25, 1885, not paginated.
[2]Ibid., Dec. 25, 1885.
[3]Solis Cohen, "J.T.S. Past and Future," p. 23.
[4]*Proceedings*, J.T.S.A., 1896, p. 30.

just completed a term as treasurer of the congregation.[5] On November 26, 1885, Morais wrote a stirring letter to Piza, entreating his support for the Seminary, and declaring that, "The best arms of defense against the men opposed to historical Judaism are faith and erudition. These cannot be acquired except in schools under the guidance and supervision of well qualified persons."[6] Piza apparently agreed to do two things on behalf of the project: to enlist the aid of the board of Shearith Israel, and to raise funds from wealthy members of the congregation. Less than three weeks later, Piza informed Morais of the earliest results of his labors:

> I brought your project before the Board of Trustees of our congregation as promised, but I regret to say that no action was taken, as they did not seem to think it practicable, or that a college would be of any use. But I do not intend to let the matter drop there. At the next meeting I shall have it brought to the vote; and in order to test the temper of the congregation, and enable the trustees to vote accordingly, I am getting three hundred copies of your letter to me printed, for distribution among the contributors to our Synagogue.[7]

With great insight, Piza told Morais that the proposed Seminary would only succeed if it were backed by a national congregational union: "I believe there are numerous such [small] congregations all over the land who wd. not refuse their mite if we had a well-organized body to reach them. I would not place all my dependence on large congregations alone, however apparently influential, but agitate in the endeavor to make the project a popular one."[8]

Among the wealthy Jewish New Yorkers whom Piza contacted was Jules A. Menken, who pinpointed exactly the financial difficulties that the Seminary was to have until its reorganization in 1902. Writing to Piza in a letter which was forwarded to Morais, Menken declared, "The serious objection to it [the Seminary] in my mind is the question of ways and means." He continued, "I think you

---

[5]David and Tamar de Sola Pool, *An Old Faith in the New World: Portrait of Shearith Israel 1654-1954* (N.Y., 1955), p. 503.

[6]Solis Cohen, "J.T.S. Past and Future," p. 16.

[7]Letter from David M. Piza to S. Morais, Dec. 15, 1885, Morais Papers.

[8]Ibid.

misunderestimate in the first place the expenses of a College . . . To make an effort at all commensurate with the evil to be counteracted some hundreds of thousands of dollars should be raised and even then it would be years ere its influence could be felt."[9] Like Piza, Menken also felt that the project would only succeed if the Seminary were backed by a union of synagogues, as was the case with the Hebrew Union College.

In addition to contacting David Piza, Alexander Kohut, and Pereira Mendes, Morais also wrote to traditional colleagues around the country, soliciting their support for the proposed seminary. Among the individuals who responded to his plea was Rabbi Bernard Drachman of Newark, who was destined to play a great role in the shaping of the early Seminary. Drachman was an American-born young man, raised in Jersey City, who had prepared for the rabbinate at the Jewish Theological Seminary of Breslau, which had been founded by Zacharias Frankel. After telling Morais that he felt "extremely honored to be asked" to participate in the project, Drachman went on to offer a suggestion: "If the proposed Rabbinical Seminary be established, I hope it will be modeled upon the Breslau Seminary at which I had the honor of [?] through my course of studies and whose methods I am convinced are the best adapted for doing justice both to the spirit of the age and of Judaism." Drachman continued, "In any event I am prepared to do all I can in the way of teaching or financial assistance"; and, somewhat apologetically, he assured Morais that he was fully orthodox, despite the fact that his congregation, Oheb Shalom, had mixed seating.[10]

Morais received added support for his Seminary proposal when his close friend and former pupil, Cyrus Adler, published an open letter in the *American Hebrew*, calling for the establishment of a "Conservative College."[11] Decrying the Pittsburgh Platform, Adler asserted, "Too long have we been deluded with the cry of peace when there was no peace—with Union when union was but a name." The recipient of a doctorate in Semitics from Johns Hopkins

---

[9]Letter from Jules A. Menken to David M. Piza, Dec. 14, 1885, Morais Papers.
[10]Letter from Bernard Drachman to S. Morais, Dec. 27, 1885, Morais Papers.
[11]*AH*, Dec. 18, 1885, p. 83.

University, Adler was currently working in the Smithsonian Institution in Washington; and, like Drachman, he was destined to play a great role in the subsequent history of the Seminary.

As the year 1886 opened, Morais's Seminary project was well under way. He came to New York to confer with Pereira Mendes; and the two men agreed that Morais would speak in Shearith Israel on the Sabbath of *Parshat Mishpatim*, at the end of January, and Mendes would address Mikveh Israel on the following Sabbath.[12] Indeed, Mendes even offered to switch synagogues with Morais, or to serve as his assistant, in order to further the growth of the Seminary, but Morais declined the very gracious offer. David Piza's efforts also bore fruit, for, on January 7, 1886, acting upon a motion made by Rev. Mendes, the Board of Trustees of Congregation Shearith Israel voted to convene a meeting for the purpose of founding a rabbinical seminary; and they stipulated that invitations should be sent to leading rabbis in the United States and Canada.[13]

The Seminary project received another great boost when it won the unqualified support of New York's leading Jewish newspaper, the *American Hebrew*. Founded in 1879 by publisher Philip Cowen (1853-1943), at the urging of Rev. Frederick de Sola Mendes, the *American Hebrew* soon became synonymous with the modern traditionalist point of view that Moshe Davis calls the "Historical School." Born in New York City to a German-Jewish family, Cowen was an ambitious and articulate printer, whose ownership of the *American Hebrew* brought him into contact with almost every major American Jewish personality in the concluding decades of the nineteenth century. The editorial board of the newspaper—which was kept secret until its thirty-third anniversary—consisted of Rev. Frederick de Sola Mendes, Rev. H. Pereira Mendes, Daniel P. Hays, Cyrus L. Sulzberger, Philip Cowen, Dr. Solomon Solis Cohen, Max Cohen, Samuel Greenbaum, and Jacob Fonseca da Silva Solis (later replaced by Cyrus Adler), almost all of whom became extremely active in Seminary affairs.[14] Indeed, the relationship between the

---

[12]Henry Pereira Mendes, "The Beginnings of the Seminary," in *The Jewish Theological Seminary of America Semi-Centennial Volume*, ed. by Cyrus Adler (N.Y., 1939), p. 38.

[13]Pool, *Old Faith*, p. 386.

[14]Cowen, *Memories*, pp. 41-43.

American Hebrew and the Seminary was so close that Isaac Mayer Wise's *American Israelite* once called its editors the "loving parents" of the new institution.[15] On January 8, 1886, the editors castigated Isaac Mayer Wise for his role in the Pittsburgh Conference. Wise, they declared,

> . . . must be held accountable. He helped to accomplish these results, and he has vehemently defended them. Those results as embodied in the resolutions which he has called expressively a Declaration of Independence, are not altogether in harmony with the principles of Judaism. These are the reasons which must urgently appeal to conservative Congregations, Reform as well as orthodox, to induce them to withdraw their moral and financial support from the Hebrew Union College, and inspire them to unite at once for the purpose of founding a Rabbinical and Hebrew Teachers' Seminary.[16]

Once again the following week, in an editorial entitled, "The Proposed Seminary," the *American Hebrew* called upon all its readers to support the new institution. The editors strongly rejected the notion that the Seminary would be orthodox; and instead they felt that it should be open to any Jew who rejected the results of the Pittsburgh Conference: "The proposed Seminary must not be identified with sectarian tendency; nor with any individual congregation . . . . This is as much antagonistic to an Orthodox Seminary, whatever that may mean, as to a Radical Reform College. What we want is a *Jewish* seminary, a Hebrew institute of learning."[17] In rejecting the idea that the Seminary should be orthodox, the editors were not only revealing their own religious bias, they were also hoping to win a greater measure of financial and moral support from the American Jewish community.

In Philadelphia, the *Jewish Record* also gave its unqualified support to the Seminary project:

> There is but one remedy left to protect American Judaism from further injury; it is by refusing moral and pecuniary support to a Jewish College governed by Dr. Wise. Conservative congregations, if they

---

[15]*American Israelite*, Sept. 3, 1886, p. 5.
[16]*AH*, Jan. 8, 1886, cover page.

desire to be consistent and not remain longer the laughing stock of the radicals, and misjudged by respectable Christians, should at once organize a union for the support of a *true* Jewish College.[18]

In the middle of January, 1886, Morais assembled an informal group of Seminary supporters in New York City, and it was resolved that he should compose a circular to be distributed to the general community, describing the aims of the new institution.[19] When the circular appeared at the end of the month, its headline was the same prayerbook quotation that Isaac Lesser had chosen as the motto of Maimonides College:

To Learn and To Teach, To Observe and To Practice

The undersigned, believing it imperative to make a strong effort for the perpetuation of historical Judaism in America, invite the cooperation of all Hebrews who share their views.

A meeting of Ministers will shortly be held to take action in this direction. It is proposed to found an institution in which Bible and Talmud shall be studied to a religious purpose. This will involve a considerable expenditure. We therefore take the liberty of forwarding to you the annexed subscription blank, to which we ask your considerable attention.

It is fondly hoped that the thought of supplying our schools and our pulpits with men broadly cultured and earnest in their adherence to their ancestral faith will incite congregations and individuals to aid with unstinted liberality an undertaking so thoroughly Jewish.

Rev. Dr. A. Kohut, New York; Rev. A.P. Mendes, Newport, R.I.; Rev. S. Morais, Phila. Pa.; Rev. Dr. F. de Sola Mendes, N.Y.; Rev. Dr. H.P. Mendes, N.Y.; Rev. Dr. B. Drachman, Newark, N.J.; Rev. Dr. H.W. Schneeberger, Baltimore, Md.[20]

---

[17]Ibid., Jan. 15, 1886, p. 4.
[18]*Jewish Record*, Dec. 11, 1885, n.p.
[19]Solis Cohen, "J.T.S. Past and Future," p. 23.
[20]Circular, Morais Collection, Annenberg Research Institute; Nussenbaum, *Champion*, pp. 109-110.

As agreed, on Shabat, January 30, Sabato Morais ascended the pulpit of Congregation Shearith Israel in New York City, and pleaded for support for his project. The following day, Sunday, January 31, 1886, the Jewish Theological Seminary was founded. As the *American Hebrew* put it so simply, "Without any parade or pretentiousness, twelve earnest representative gentlemen met in the trustee room of the Shearith Israel synagogue, last Sunday afternoon, and founded a college of instruction in conservative Jewish principles."[21] Attending the conference were Rev. A.P. Mendes of Newport, R.I.; Revs. S. Morais and J. Chumaceiro of Philadelphia; Rev. H. Schneeberger of Baltimore; Rev. B. Drachman of Newark; and Revs. A. Kohut, A. Wise, F. de Sola Mendes, and H. P. Mendes of New York, along with three interested laymen, "Messrs. Weil, Davidson, and Meyer."[22] At the meeting, Morais was elected chairman, and Henry Pereira Mendes was chosen as secretary. The highlight of the conference was the unanimous adoption of a resolution presented by Rev. A.P. Mendes of Newport: "Resolved that it is indispensable to the welfare and progress of Judaism in this country that there should be founded a seminary for the training of teachers of the future generation in sympathy with the spirit of Conservative Judaism, to be called, 'The Jewish Theological Seminary of New York.'"[23]

The conference was not without controversy, for both Alexander Kohut and Aaron Wise wished to omit entirely the reference to "Conservative Judaism," which, to them, apparently typecast the Seminary as an orthodox institution, and might very well prevent moderate Reformers from supporting it. Nevertheless, Sabato Morais strongly insisted upon its inclusion, and the term "Conservative Judaism" was retained.[24] Apparently there were no hard feelings, for Rev. Wise graciously offered to endow the Seminary with a comprehensive library. Among the other resolutions, it was decided to issue a circular inviting congregational rep-

---

[21]*AH*, Feb. 5, 1886, pp. 8-9.

[22]Ibid., pp. 8-9. Exactly who these laymen were cannot be determined; Mr. Weil is probably Jonas Weil, later a Seminary trustee, and father-in-law of Bernard Drachman.

[23]Ibid., pp. 8-9; *Jewish Record*, Feb. 5, 1886, n.p.

[24]*Jewish Record*, Feb. 5, 1886, n.p.

resentatives to an organizational meeting on March 7, and Revs. de Sola Mendes, H.P. Mendes, and Drachman were appointed a committee to make plans for the constitution and incorporation of the institution. In particular, the delegates resolved to make a special appeal for support to congregations in New York, Philadelphia, and Baltimore, in preparation for opening the Seminary in October, 1886.

After the January conference, the backers of the Seminary intensified their efforts to win support for the new institution. From Philadelphia, Dr. Solomon Solis Cohen wrote a long letter to the *American Hebrew* in praise of traditional Judaism and in support of the Seminary. Solis Cohen, a close friend and student of Sabato Morais, was an extraordinarily learned layman, a gifted poet who became known for his sensitive translations of medieval Hebrew verse. His letter is remarkable because it shows what the term "traditional" meant to an intelligent, Americanized lay supporter of the Seminary. Speaking of the Seminary's traditionalist outlook, the eloquent physician declared,

> It is the only Jewish platform. But this platform does not oppose progress. Men change, times change. Customs must change in harmonious development. The laws are fixed but they are principles, not applications. As surroundings change, the application of fixed principles changes to meet its environment. It is like a revolving wheel. The circumference moves ceaselessly, but the centre is fixed, and cannot be disturbed without destroying the whole. The spokes connect the moving circumference with the fixed centre. These are the lines of interpretation and adaptation—but they are definite lines adopted by mathematical rule, and not at random and by caprice. So must the lines of interpretation of Divine law follow the definite rules of rabbinical tradition. Obedience to law, harmonious development and in accordance with traditional rules—these are the principles to be taught in the Jewish Seminary.[25]

The following week, the *American Hebrew* published another remarkable document—a sermon in support of the Seminary delivered by Sabato Morais to Congregation Chizuk Amuno of

---

[25]*AH*, Feb. 12, 1886, p. 4.

Baltimore, whose rabbi, H. W. Schneeberger, was an active backer of the new institution. In addition to the usual appeal for funds, Morais clearly set forth his academic goals for the Seminary: "the proposed seminary shall vindicate the right of the Hebrew Bible to a precedence over all theological studies. It shall be the boast of that institute hereafter that the attendants are surpassing Scripturalists—if I may be permitted the expression—though they may not rank foremost among skilled Talmudists. The latter have, at times, degenerated into hair splitting disputants—*pilpulists.*"[26] In this sermon, it can be clearly seen that Morais's image of the Seminary was very different from that of an Eastern European-style *yeshiva*, where the study of the Talmud took precedence over all. Inasmuch as curriculum is a direct reflection of philosophy, it is apparent that Morais's approach to the Jewish tradition was far more broad than that generally held by his Eastern European contemporaries.

As plans for the Seminary were concretized, it was only natural that Isaac Mayer Wise and his Reform cohorts should cry out in anger and in protest. Wise's essential approach, as expressed in the pages of the *American Israelite*, was to assert that the Seminary project was a complete fraud—it was to be an orthodox seminary founded by non-orthodox men, merely for the purpose of opposing him and the Hebrew Union College. On March 12, 1886, Wise unleashed his attack:

> The New York-Philadelphia opposition to the Hebrew Union College and the 'Union' sends a circular to all supposed orthodox people, begging support for the establishment of an orthodox Rabbinical seminary, and there are two mistakes in that business, viz., the circulars are sent to parties who have no idea of assisting in that enterprise. . ., and in the second place the designers of the circulars are no orthodox men, so that none who know them will believe them to be in earnest in regard to establishing an orthodox Rabbinical seminary. The genuinely orthodox congregations . . .will certainly have nothing to do with men who are engaged, and under salaries, in so-called reform congregations and maintain they are building up an orthodox seminary.[27]

---

[26]Ibid., Feb. 19, 1886, pp. 3-4.
[27]*American Israelite*, March 12, 1886, p. 4.

While Wise was willing to concede that there was a need for a truly orthodox seminary, and he himself would support it just "to get rid of the opposition," he felt that,

> Few, however, will have much money to spend for a mere opposition seminary, to be called orthodox, under the auspices of men who are themselves *Poshim* in the eyes not only of the genuines of Poland and Hungary, but also of the leaders of that class in Germany and Italy. The only orthodox man in that scheme is an Italian Hazan, who, God bless his soul, is unable to perpetrate a fraud otherwise, and appears in this connection as a deceived deceiver.

In asserting that the Seminary was to be an orthodox institution, Wise was employing an adjective that the founders of the Seminary consciously avoided, probably due to the insistence and the participation of Alexander Kohut. In an article entitled, "The Jewish Seminary," published in the *American Hebrew* and the *Jewish Record*, Kohut projected his non-denominational vision of the new institution:

> Reform, conservatism, orthodoxy—these are the watchwords under which the verbal battle is fought, and the result is that the pure faith cannot obtain its due acknowledgment. Therefore, we imperiously need a seminary which shall have no other ambition, and no other title than that it be purely and truly Jewish. We do not desire it to be destined for a sect, whether reform, conservative, or orthodox, we would have it be a Jewish theological seminary, like that of Breslau, for example.[28]

As we have seen, from the very beginning, the Seminary won the support of men such as Marcus Jastrow, Benjamin Szold, and Dr. Kohut, who were clearly not orthodox, but who strongly rejected the antinomian tendencies of Isaac Mayer Wise. Wise's theory was very simple: either you were 100% orthodox or you were not orthodox at all, and if you were not, you had no right to oppose the Hebrew Union College, which provided a traditional Jewish education and allowed the students to fashion their own theology. Clearly

---

[28]*AH*, Feb. 5, 1886, pp. 2-3.

Wise did not accept the existence of an "Historical School"; and if he did somehow grasp the notion that a third party was slowly taking shape in American Judaism, he was certainly not willing to lend it legitimacy by recognizing its seminary.

Although the greatest source of opposition to the Seminary project was the Reform movement, led by Isaac Mayer Wise, the Eastern European orthodox Jewish community was skeptical as well. The early Seminary leaders did, indeed, make an effort to enlist the support of their "downtown" brethren, and to a limited degree, they were successful. Nevertheless, to some of the more extreme orthodox, the Seminary was "treyf" from the very beginning, because it actively solicited the aid of moderate Reform rabbis and congregations, and because of the leadership role that Alexander Kohut was taking in the new enterprise. As we have seen, the orthodox scholar, J.D. Eisenstein, was among the first writers to use the term "Conservative" precisely in the sense that it is used today. In an 1886 article written in the *New Yorker Yidishe Zeitung*, entitled "Founding of the New Seminary," Eisenstein declared, "In my opinion, the objective of Conservatism and the law of the Radicals lead to the same path, the only difference between them is the time," namely, that the Conservatives go more slowly in making changes.[29] Under the rubric "Conservative," Eisenstein condemned not only Alexander Kohut, for serving in a synagogue that had made many reforms in the liturgy, but also Sabato Morais, because he was lukewarm towards the restoration of the sacrifices.

Like Isaac Mayer Wise, therefore, Eisenstein felt that there were only two possible options for American Judaism—Reform and Orthodoxy. Using the language of the Bible, he declared, "To the Conservatives, I call, 'how long halt ye between two opinions'! [I Kings 18.21, J.P.S. trans.]. If your faith is orthodox, follow it, and if it is Radical, follow after it."[30] Thus, for Eisenstein, the proposed Seminary would only be worthy of support if its founders would completely renounce their ties to Reform Judaism. In order to merit the support of the orthodox, Eisenstein declared that the Seminary must accept four basic principles: 1. The Seminary founders should

---

[29]Eisenstein, *Ozar Zikhronothai*, p. 208.
[30]Ibid., p. 209.

accept no help from Reform congregations, lest they take over; 2. The teachers and lay leaders must be fully observant Jews; 3. The students should study with covered heads and not learn anything contrary to the *Shulchan Aruch*; 4. The first students should be between six and eight years old, and should pursue their secular, as well as Jewish, studies at the institution, so as not to be influenced by the public schools.[31]

Needless to say, neither the criticism of Wise nor of Eisenstein had much effect upon the Seminary leadership; and both Morais and Kohut continued their efforts to gain a wide-spread base of support for the new institution. Towards the end of February, 1886, Alexander Kohut "addressed a gathering in Essex Street . . . where representatives from 136 congregations, chevaras and other societies were present. They all promised to interest their constituents and felt quite assured that they would all aid the movement."[32] As we shall see in a later chapter, the Seminary's efforts to recruit "downtown" support came largely to naught, not only because of the religious, social, and economic differences between the J.T.S. leaders and the "East Siders," but also because the Yeshivat Etz Chaim was founded at approximately the same time in New York City, and tended to draw financial support away from the Seminary. Offering an all-day program chiefly consisting of Jewish studies, Yeshivat Etz Chaim was a conscious attempt to establish an Eastern European-style *yeshiva* on the Lower East Side. In a further effort to gain financial support for his project, Sabato Morais wrote to "some acquaintances abroad—men intelligent and wealthy," but, unfortunately, "none agreed to assist."[33]

In the aftermath of the January 31 organizational meeting, the Seminary leadership sent out invitations to congregations around the country, inviting them to a meeting at Shearith Israel in New York on Sunday, March, 7, 1886. Two days before the meeting, the *American Hebrew* published a rousing editorial in favor of the Seminary, declaring that it was the duty of every Jew to help spark "a Hebrew Renaissance" in the United States by supporting the

---

[31]Ibid., p. 211.

[32]*AH*, March 5, 1886, p. 9; *Jewish Record*, March 5, 1886, n.p.

[33]S. Morais, untitled, undated essay on Gratz College, Morais Papers.

Seminary; and it especially called upon "our men of wealth to demonstrate that their views of philanthropy are not confined to alms-giving, but are as broad as the spread of culture."[34]

The meeting itself was a great success. At least twenty-two synagogues were represented: nine from New York, five from Boston, two from Baltimore, and one each from Philadelphia, New Haven, Richmond, Newport, Jersey City, and Newark; and letters of support were also received from synagogues in Philadelphia, New York, Boston and Cleveland.[35] Most of these congregations were highly Americanized, traditional synagogues, but it is interesting to note that the Beth Hamedrash Hagadol, New York's premier Eastern European orthodox congregation, also sent a representative. Among the more prominent individuals attending the meeting were Revs. Morais, Schneeberger, A.P. Mendes, H.P. Mendes, F. de Sola Mendes, Drachman, A. Wise, and Moses Maisner, as well as the prominent lay leaders, Joseph Blumenthal, J. Edgar Phillips, Cyrus Sulzberger, and Dr. Solomon Solis Cohen. Alexander Kohut was unable to attend because he was in mourning for his wife, Julia.

The meeting was called to order by J. Edgar Phillips, a wealthy leader of Shearith Israel, the host congregation; and shortly thereafter Dr. Solomon Solis Cohen was elected chairman, and Rev. H.P. Mendes was chosen secretary. The main business of the meeting was to ratify the new constitution for the association, which was henceforth to be called the "Jewish Theological Seminary Association," dropping the phrase, "of New York." Although the constitution presentation committee consisted of Revs. Drachman, F. de Sola Mendes, and H.P. Mendes, the document had been carefully written by Dr. Solis Cohen, and then approved by the rabbis prior to the meeting.[36]

---

[34]*AH*, March 5, 1886, p. 2.

[35]Ibid., March 12, 1886, p. 10. Elsewhere in the same issue, the *AH* asserts that "some sixty congregations" were represented, and, the following week, March 19, the paper asserts that "about" 38 synagogues sent delegates (p.10), contradicting a letter from Rev. H. P. Mendes, who put the number at 25. Since Mendes was the secretary of the meeting, his figure is probably reasonably accurate.

[36]Solis Cohen, "J.T.S. Past and Future," p. 25.

The preamble to the constitution carefully sets forth the founders' vision of the new Seminary:

> The necessity having been made manifest for associated and organized efforts on the part of the Jews of America faithful to Mosaic law and ancestral tradition, for the purpose of keeping alive the true Judaic spirit, and in particular the establishment of a seminary, where the Bible shall be impartially taught and rabbinical literature faithfully expounded, and more especially, where youths desirous of entering the ministry may be thoroughly grounded in Jewish knowledge and inspired by the precept and example of their instructors with the love of the Hebrew language and a spirit of fidelity and devotion to the Jewish law, in accordance with a resolution adopted at a meeting of ministers held January 31, 1886, at the Shearith Israel Synagogue of the City of New York, the subscribers have agreed to organize the Jewish Theological Seminary Association.[37]

Article II of the document goes into even greater detail in presenting the goals of the founders:

> The purpose of this Association being the preservation in America of the knowledge and practice of historical Judaism as ordained in the Law of Moses and expounded by the prophets and sages of Israel in Biblical and Talmudical writings, it proposes in the furtherance of its general aim, the following specific objects.
> 1. The establishment and maintenance of a Jewish theological seminary for the training of rabbis and teachers.
> 2. The attainment of such cognate purposes as may upon occasion be deemed appropriate.

With regard to the rather cryptic phrase, "such cognate purposes as may upon occasion be deemed appropriate," Solomon Solis Cohen years later wrote that he included this ambiguous passage in the constitution because he hoped that the institution might one day develop into a "Jewish University in America . . . with the Seminary as its Divinity School."[38]

---

[37] *AH*, March 12, 1886, p. 10; *Jewish Record*, March 12, 1886, n.p.
[38] Solis Cohen, "J.T.S. Past and Future," p. 43.

To provide financial support for the Seminary, various membership categories were established: Subscribers were to pay $5 a year;
Patrons, $10 a year; Life members, $100; and Life Patrons, $200. For
the purposes of conventions, synagogues with less than twenty-five
members were entitled to one delegate, for $15 a year. With more
than twenty-five members, a congregation would be entitled to one
delegate for each $25 paid, up to a maximum of ten delegates.[39] In
addition to the usual officers, affairs of the institution were to be
conducted by a board of trustees of fifteen members. After appointing a committee to oversee the publication and distribution of the
constitution, the meeting was adjourned.

In the meanwhile, Morais and Mendes actively devoted themselves to fund-raising for the new institution; and Mendes published an open letter, "To the Jews of America," asking for support.[40] Although the financial figures for the first few months were
never made public, the response was far from overwhelming.
Shearith Israel gave $1,000—an amount that the *American Israelite*
ridiculed as a "comparatively paltry sum"[41]—a few wealthy individuals, such as the Piza family, gave sizeable donations, and the
rest of the money arrived in rather small amounts. Venting his frus-
tration, Morais declared, "Vast means are absolutely necessary.
They must be procured: not by promises, which for a variety of motives, may go unperformed, but by tangible, actual gifts of fifties,
hundreds and thousands. Then and then only will the theological
Seminary have a permanent realization."[42] Throughout its entire
history, the early Seminary was haunted by financial problems; and
although the intake of cash was steady, it was never quite adequate
to foster the growth of the institution.

In the middle of April, 1886, the Seminary leadership issued a
circular "to the Hebrews of America," inviting the public to the
election meeting of the new institution, to be held on May 9 at
Shearith Israel on 19th Street. The document is most remarkable, because it deals with the theme of the Americanization of the

---

[39]*Jewish Record*, March 12, 1886. n.p.

[40]Ibid., March 19, 1886, n.p.

[41]*American Israelite*, June 4, 1886, p. 5.

[42]S. Morais, sermon, "On the Strike, on the Ministerial Conference of May
3rd, on the Meeting for the Seminary, May 9th, '86," Morais Papers.

"Russian" immigrants, which was to play an even greater role in Seminary thinking after the arrival of Solomon Schechter. In essence, the Seminary leaders of 1886 were saying that the institution should be supported because it would help to "civilize" the new immigrants, and prevent them from becoming a source of embarrassment to the rest of American Jewry. The circular, therefore, is an excellent example of the subconscious—and sometimes conscious—snobbishness that the older Jewish community often displayed towards the new arrivals:

> Honor or shame will be attached to the Jewish name, according as these communities develop. If they do not become a source of honor, and of strength by forwarding the true interests of our faith, and gaining the esteem of the world for its followers [sic]. To secure these ends our congregations throughout the States must be provided with rabbis and teachers who will enjoy the confidence of the flock entrusted to their care, and at the same time will be able to command the respect of Jew and Christian for our religion by respecting it themselves. In both congregational and communal work the influence of cultured ministers, faithful to our religion, learned in our law, and endowed with University education, cannot be overestimated. By their intelligent efforts, they will raise the standard of their congregation, by their educational labors with the young people and children they will foster love and respect for Judaism in the next generation, and by their own consistent and religious life they will set a proper example of devotion to the faith for which our ancestors labored and died. To train such ministers, the Jewish Theological Seminary Association has been established in New York. Combined with the education necessary for a Rabbi, will be a University Course at Columbia College or the University of the City of New York [N.Y.U.].[43]

A few days before the May meeting, Alexander Kohut's congregation, Ahavath Chesed of New York, announced that it was joining the Seminary Association, while retaining its membership in the U.A.H.C. To the editors of the *American Hebrew* this seemed like a good idea, for, "there is no need of the colleges in this city and in

---

[43]*AH*, April 23, 1886, p. 9.

Cincinnati being antagonistic. The latter will continue to provide for the instruction of Western youths, while the one in New York will do the same for Eastern youths. It is simply ridiculous to go to the unnecessary expense of sending boys from New York to Cincinnati."[44] Nevertheless, although a few congregations, such as those of Szold and Jastrow, followed suit, in general, the synagogues that supported the Seminary were not affiliated with the Union.

At the May 9 meeting, at least seventeen congregations were represented, twelve from New York, two from Baltimore, and one each from Philadelphia, Pittsburgh, and Newark. The fifteen trustees were elected, and among them were such distinguished leaders as Solomon Solis Cohen, Newman Cowen, Dr. Aaron Friedenwald, Joseph Newberger, Joseph Blumenthal, David Piza, J.E. Phillips, and J.M. Emanuel, the latter four being influential members of Shearith Israel. Although no transcript of this meeting has been preserved, it apparently was subject to the usual amount of politicking and personal rivalries that almost every organization endures, for in a sermon delivered the following week, Morais lamented,

> I confess that the meeting did not fulfill my anticipations. Too much eagerness was displayed by some to gain posts of honor, and too little in sacrificing personal and congregational jealousies for the sake of the cause. Much time was frittered away, whereas it ought to have been seized upon and utilized to a righteous purpose. But what was lost can be recovered.[45]

Another negative assessment of the meeting came from the New York correspondent of the *American Israelite*. After chiding Shearith Israel for not being more generous, he went on to state that he saw no value in the Seminary's attempts to reach out to the Lower East Side. The Russian immigrants would most likely not accept the Seminary for religious reasons, but even if they did accept it, they

---

[44]Ibid., May 7, 1886, cover page.

[45]S. Morais, sermon "On the . . . Meeting for the Seminary, May 9th, '86," Morais Papers.

certainly would not help to support it. In typical "uptown" fashion, he ridiculed two East Siders who attended the conference:

> This pair, though careful in bringing with them two pairs of cork-screw like *peyes*, left their pocket-books behind them . . . This, I hope, will verify my previous assertion in the *American Israelite*, that our Russian friends, God bless them, are deserving the thanks of the community for leading the van in supplying with families our various benevolent institutions. But when it comes to supporting them they contribute phrases from the Talmud as a substitute.[46]

Instead of spending money on the Seminary, therefore, the writer suggested that the funds would be far better utilized if they were given to the Hebrew Technical Institute or the Hebrew Union College.

In response, the editors of the *American Hebrew* lambasted this point of view, declaring that there was no reason why the different segments of New York Jewry could not work together for the good of the Seminary: "an actual union of the east side and down town Jews with their up town brethren in the support of a great educational institution would be the most important event in Jewish circles in the last quarter of a century."[47]

One week after the election meeting, on Sunday, May 16, the board held its first meeting and elected the following officers: President, Joseph Blumenthal; Vice President, Dr. Aaron Friedenwald; Treasurer, Newman Cowen; and Secretary, Joseph Newberger.[48] Each of these men was distinguished in both the Jewish and general communities; and they would surely lend prestige to the new institution. Blumenthal had served as a member of the New York State Assembly and had also been a member of the "Committee of Seventy" that helped bring down the Tweed Ring.[49] He had served as President of Shearith Israel in 1882-83, and was also active in the Y.M.H.A. and in B'nai B'rith. Friedenwald was a very distinguished physician in Baltimore and was extremely active

---

[46]*American Israelite*, June 4, 1886, p. 5.
[47]*AH*, June 25, 1886, pp. 2-3.
[48]*Jewish Record*, May 21, 1886, p. 5.
[49]Pool, *Old Faith*, p. 318.

in Jewish community affairs on both a local and a national level, later serving as Vice President of the Federation of American Zionists. Representing the East Side was Newman Cowen, who "was the first Russian-Polish Jew that arrived here who became a factor in the life of the community."[50] A successful businessman, Cowen was also a learned Talmudist and a devout Jew, known for his philanthropy on the Lower East Side. Newberger was a trustee of Congregation Rodef Sholom in New York, president of District #1 of B'nai B'rith, and was later chosen to serve as a judge in the City Court of New York.

At the end of June, 1886, another meeting, exclusively for rabbis, was held at Shearith Israel for the purpose of planning the academic policies and the curriculum of the Seminary; and Drs. Kohut and Pereira Mendes were appointed to confer with the trustees on these matters.[51] The newly-elected trustees of the Seminary also kept busy that summer, holding their business meetings at Long Branch, the "Jewish Newport" on the Jersey Shore, where several of them owned large summer mansions.[52] It was in Long Branch that the trustees adopted the policy of using a "quiet method" to build support for the Seminary, perhaps so as to avoid open condemnation by Wise and the Union; but, in a rare outburst of criticism, the *American Hebrew* later chided the trustees for this policy, stating that more publicity was necessary for the new institution.[53]

As plans for the opening of the Seminary progressed rather slowly—the October opening date had to be postponed, the *American Israelite* stepped up its attacks, stating that the institution would never succeed, that it would never raise enough money, and that the Eastern European orthodox would never support it because of the presence of Dr. Kohut. In September, Wise's paper arrogantly crowed about "the defeated seminary"; it has failed because people "see that that seminary business is rotten to the core. The cornerstone is laid upon hatred, jealousy, and conceit to wreck its [sic] present noble institute, the Cincinnati College."[54]

---

[50]Cowen, *Memories*, p. 23; Philip Cowen was a distant cousin to Newman.
[51]*AH*, June 25, 1886, p. 9.
[52]*American Israelite*, July 23, 1886, p. 4.
[53]*AH*, Oct. 15, 1886. p. 2.
[54]*American Israelite*, Sept. 3, 1886, p. 5.

Nevertheless, despite the criticism and the pessimism of Isaac
Mayer Wise, the Seminary leaders steadfastly persisted in their attempts to open the institution. At a trustees' meeting late in October,
Max Cohen, who would serve the institution well for many years,
was elected assistant secretary; and it was also resolved to issue a
circular, to be sent to all American congregations, setting forth the
purposes of the Seminary and a rough outline of its curriculum.
Shortly thereafter, another announcement was released, presenting
the admission standards for the Seminary and requesting all
prospective students to apply to Secretary Joseph E. Newberger in
New York. In order to enter the Preparatory Department of the
Seminary, students were required to know "Bible History to Ezra
(chief events), Religious observances (festivals, etc.), easy Hebrew
Grammar, and translations of simple passages from the Pentateuch
and prayer book."[55] Not coincidentally, these requirements were almost identical to the admission standards of the Hebrew Union
College.[56]

A public examination for prospective students was held on
Sunday, November 21, 1886; and the aspiring scholars had to face
questions from Revs. Morais, F. de Sola Mendes, A. Wise, H.P.
Mendes, and Drachman, as well as from Joseph Blumenthal and
Solomon Solis Cohen. Seven students applied for admission: five
were American-born, and several were already in college.[57] On
December 17, another examination was held, and six more students
applied for admission. Of the thirteen students who applied, eight
were admitted immediately, and the other five were held in
abeyance, pending their further mastery of the English language.[58]

In December, 1886, the trustees named an Advisory Board of
Ministers, consisting of Revs. Sabato Morais, Henry S. Jacobs (of
Congregation B'nai Jeshurun), Alexander Kohut, Frederick de Sola
Mendes, H. Pereira Mendes, Aaron Wise, Henry W. Schneeberger,
and Bernard Drachman; and shortly thereafter Morais was elected
president of this board. With the students having been admitted, the

[55]*AH*, Nov. 19, 1886, p. 9.
[56]*American Israelite*, August 10, 1883, p. 4.
[57]*AH*, Nov. 26, 1886, p. 2.
[58]Ibid., Jan. 7, 1887, p. 2.

members of the Advisory Board volunteered to serve as the faculty—an arrangement that did not last; and Shearith Israel offered the use of its vestry room for classes. With great pride, the trustees of the new institution invited the public to the formal opening exercises, to be held at Lyric Hall on Sixth Avenue near 42nd Street on January 2, 1887; and on that day, the Jewish Theological Seminary became a reality.

Reverend Sabato Morais
Courtesy of the Library of the Jewish Theological Seminary of America

Reverend Henry Pereira Mendes
Courtesy of the Library of the Jewish Theological Seminary of America

Rabbi Alexander Kohut
Courtesy of the Library of the Jewish Theological Seminary of America

Rabbi Bernard Drachman
Courtesy of the Library of the Jewish Theological Seminary of America

Hon. Joseph Blumenthal
Courtesy of the Jewish Theological Seminary of America

Dr. Solomon Solis Cohen
Courtesy of the Library of the Jewish Theological Seminary of America

Rabbi Joseph H. Hertz upon his graduation from the Seminary
Courtesy of the American Jewish Historical Society

Professor Joshua Joffe and his pupil friends, 1897
Courtesy of the Jewish Theological Seminary of America

first row (left to right): Leon H. Elmaleh, David Levine, Professor Joffe, Herman Abramowitz, Charles H. Kauvar.
second row: Elias L. Solomon, Mordecai M. Kaplan, Alter Abelson, Morris Mandel, Nathan Wolf.
third row: Menahem M. Eichler, Michael Fried, Bernard Ehrenreich, Bernard Kaplan, Julius Greenstone.

Identification: Davis, Emergence, opp. p. 243.

CHAPTER IV

Academic Aspects of the Early Seminary

T he crowd that assembled in New York's Lyric Hall on
January 2, 1887, for the opening exercises of the Jewish
Theological Seminary could not have foreseen that the
institution would be vibrant and thriving as it begins its second
century. What must have attracted the attention of knowledgeable
observers, however, was the unique coalition of rabbis that made
the birth of the Seminary possible, as well as the varied rabbinical
personalities who were present for the ceremony itself. The leading
speakers for the occasion were Revs. Sabato Morais and Alexander
Kohut, representing the right and left wings of the so-called
"Historical School." Also present were Revs. Drachman, Pereira
Mendes, Jacobs, de Sola Mendes, Maisner, and Aaron Wise; and a
special guest was Rabbi Gustav Gottheil, the venerable leader of
New York's foremost Reform synagogue, Temple Emanu-El, who
had graciously come to give the new institution his blessing. To see
a group of rabbis with such varying outlooks, all assembled for the
very same purpose, was indeed a rarity in the 1880's; and yet it was
precisely this religious pluralism that was to be the hallmark of the
Seminary for the next one hundred years.

Rev. Henry Pereira Mendes opened the program with a prayer
for the Seminary, after which President Joseph Blumenthal spoke
about the need for funds, calling upon the public to provide a
$100,000 endowment for the new institution. Next, Dr. Kohut rose to
speak; and apparently attempting to placate the members of the
U.A.H.C. who felt that his Reform congregation should have
nothing to do with the Seminary, he insisted that this was not to be
an "opposition Seminary," and that he had only best wishes for the
Hebrew Union College. Nevertheless, he insisted that a Seminary
was necessary for the Jews of the East, which was rapidly becoming
the center of American Judaism. Naturally, almost everyone in the

audience knew that this was indeed to be an "opposition Seminary"; and, if there were any doubts, they were certainly dispelled by his address:

> In the new Seminary a different spirit will prevail, different impulses will pervade its teachings and animate its teachers. This spirit shall be that of *Conservative* Judaism, the *conserving* Jewish impulse which will create in the pupils of the Seminary the tendency to recognize the dual nature of Judaism and the Law; which unites theory and practice, identifies body and the soul, realizes the importance of both matter and spirit, and acknowledges the necessity of observing the Law as well as studying it.[1]

When Dr. Morais was called upon to speak, once again he stressed the importance that Biblical studies were to play in the curriculum of the Seminary. Promising that "the atmosphere pervading it shall be purely Jewish," Morais went on to assert that the irreverent, destructive, so-called "higher criticism," very much in vogue at that time, would play no part in the Seminary's course of study:

> I do not presume too much when I declare in the name of its founders, that the icy cold criticism of the German and Dutch schools of modern times shall not be permitted to blight the growth of religious enthusiasm in the hearts of our pupils . . . Never will we suffer an exegesis, as un-Jewish as it is insidious, aye, murderous to our creed, to convert our trained defenders into compromising foes.[2]

In publicly rejecting higher Biblical criticism as an object of study at the Seminary, Morais was not only attempting to pacify the Eastern European orthodox, who were somewhat suspicious of the Seminary due to the participation of Alexander Kohut, he was also reflecting the view held by many Jews in the nineteenth century that biblical criticism was a covert form of anti-Semitism.

In addition to the addresses of Kohut and Morais, the audience also heard words of encouragement from Rabbi Henry S. Jacobs of

---

[1]*AH*, Jan. 7, 1887. p. 8.
[2]Ibid., Jan. 7, 1887. pp. 4-5.

Congregation B'nai Jeshurun in New York and from Rabbi Bernard Drachman of Newark. After a benediction by Rev. Morais, President Blumenthal concluded the ceremony.

The following day, January 3, 1887, in the vestry room of Congregation Shearith Israel, the Seminary held its first classes. That first Preparatory Class consisted of eight students—William Kurtz, Israel Cohn, Joseph H. Hertz, Emanuel Hertz (Joseph's brother), Solomon Bernstein, Samuel Seiniger, Hyman Simson, and Raymond Rubenstein.[3] At least three of these young men had been born in New York. As we shall see, the students were all very poor, the course of study was difficult; and, for a variety of reasons, of the original students, only Joseph Hertz went on to graduate from the Seminary. They were all very young; and the six for whom we have records ranged in age from thirteen to fifteen.[4] Although we have no record of what year they attended in secular school, within one year, five of them were attending C.C.N.Y. In February, the Advisory Board conducted further examinations for admission, and by March the Preparatory Class had increased to fourteen students, who had already formed their own "literary society."[5]

Initially the classes were taught by the rabbis of the Advisory Board, but in February, 1887, Dr. Bernard Drachman was hired to teach the Preparatory Class. A native-born American, educated at Columbia University, Drachman had prepared for the rabbinate at the Jewish Theological Seminary of Breslau. In 1886, shortly after the Seminary Association was founded, Sabato Morais had approached Drachman about teaching at the institution; and, after an "informal examination" in Jewish studies, Morais made the proposal concrete.[6]

As a native-born American, a traditionalist, and a congregational rabbi in nearby Newark, Drachman was ideally suited for a position at the Seminary, One of the charges that the Reformers always levelled at the traditionalists in the nineteenth century was the allegation that they were out of step with American life, and that

---

[3]Ibid., p. 137.
[4]*Proceedings*, J.T.S.A., 1888, p. 17.
[5]*AH*, Feb. 18, 1887, cover page.
[6]Drachman, *Light*, p . 182 .

they were a throwback to Europe. Thus, having a man with Drachman's qualifications on the faculty could only serve to build up the image of the Seminary, as well as of traditional American Judaism in general. In the spring of 1887, Drachman left Newark and accepted a position at Congregation Beth Israel Bikur Cholim on 72nd Street and Lexington Avenue in New York, thereby making him even more accessible to the Seminary. Drachman later resigned from the congregation over the issue of mixed seating, which he now strongly opposed, and became rabbi of Congregation Zichron Ephraim in 1889.[7]

The students in the first year of the Seminary studied a truly varied curriculum, attending classes five days a week for two hours after the conclusion of their secular school day. By June of the first year, they had covered five chapters of Genesis, along with Rashi's commentary, selections from the Psalms, with special attention devoted to syntax and grammar, as well as an introduction to Biblical History. In Rabbinics, they had covered part of the Mishnah of Berachot, with the commentary of Bartinura, as well as selections from the Gemara of Bava Metzia. In his report to the Seminary Board, Dr. Morais lamented, "We might have preferred that the Babylonian Gemara upon the same treatise [Berachot] should have been used to gradually familiarize the pupils with Talmudical language and debates, but the impossibility of procuring all the copies needed compelled the selection of *Baba Metzia*."[8] At the end of June, the Seminary Advisory Board conducted a public examination of the students, as was the custom of the day.[9] A large crowd attended, and the general consensus was that the students had made great progress.

Although the students were compelled to study through the summer, it was not all hard work. One sunny day in July, they sailed for 2 1/2 hours to Long Branch, along with Drs. Drachman and Pereira Mendes, where they were entertained at the summer mansion of Mr. J.M. Emanuel, a Seminary trustee. As the *American*

---

[7]Ibid., pp. 200-207.

[8]*AH*, July 1, 1887, p. 8.

[9]H.U.C. and later the Rabbi Isaac Elchanan Theological Seminary did the same, often inviting distinguished rabbis to serve as examiners.

Hebrew noted, "In the afternoon the boys enjoyed a game of base-ball in thoroughly hearty and genuine American style."[10] After dedicating Mr. Emanuel's new house, and praying the afternoon service in his private synagogue, the boys sailed home to New York, "having spent a most pleasant and agreeable day."

Although the Reform movement gradually came to accept the existence of the Seminary as inevitable, in the summer of 1887, a very heated literary controversy broke out between Dr. Solomon Solis Cohen of the Seminary Board, and Dr. Richard Gottheil, a Columbia professor who was the son of Rabbi Gustav Gottheil of Temple Emanu-El. The controversy began when Solis Cohen published an article in the *American Hebrew* entitled "Under Which Flag," in which he condemned the Hebrew Union College for embarking on a fund-raising campaign just at the time when the Seminary was trying to raise $100,000 for an endowment fund:

> But now comes a counter appeal from the college at Cincinnati for five hundred thousand dollars to continue its work of destruction; to enable it to train ministers to throw ridicule upon the laws of Moses; to overturn the labor of the prophets, to trample underfoot the hedges of the Sages. Let those who are tired of Judaism, and wish to see the religion of their fathers destroyed, respond liberally to the appeal.[11]

Raising the pitch of his argument, Solis Cohen defied the Reformers, whom he called "prophets of Baal," to either accept the Law or become Christians, deciding under which flag they would march.

In response, Gottheil asserted that the traditionalists had done almost nothing for the American Jewish community; all the fine Jewish charitable institutions in this country had been started by Reform Jews. The Seminary, he asserted, would "turn out Jesuitical, narrow-minded, fanatical teachers of religion"; and he proclaimed, "I declare it to be a crying wrong that one cent of money should be given to this hotbed of exclusiveness and of down-right bigotry."[12]

The controversy, dubbed the "War of the Doctors," raged throughout the summer of 1887 in the pages of the *American Hebrew*,

---

[10]*AH*, July 15, 1887, p. 8.
[11]Ibid., July 22, 1887, p. 3.
[12]Ibid., July 29, 1887, p. 3.

with Henry Pereira Mendes coming to the defense of Solis Cohen, and Kaufmann Kohler supporting Gottheil. Perhaps the most sensible words uttered in the entire episode came from an anonymous letter-writer from Washington, D.C.—probably Cyrus Adler—who asserted that there was room for both colleges in the American Jewish community: "Yer pays yer money, yer takes yer choice . . . It is our boast that we are charitable in *deed*. Why then should we not be charitable in *thought*?"[13] As cooler heads prevailed, the controversy came to an end, but it left a residue of hard feelings that could only serve to hurt the Seminary's hopes of raising support from the moderate Reform elements of American Jewry.

In October, 1887, the Seminary left Shearith Israel and moved to Cooper Union, at 8th Street and Fourth Avenue, where it rented rooms for four years. Shortly thereafter, the Seminary board advertised for candidates for a "higher department"; and by December, a Junior Class had been formed. The Seminary's enrollment now stood at nineteen—twelve students in the Preparatory Class and seven in the Junior;[14] and it was necessary for the trustees to hire another instructor, Dr. Gustave Lieberman, who taught Mishnah and Gemara. Although we do not have any information on Dr. Lieberman's academic background, it is known that he was born in Hungary and came to American with his five children after his business ventures had failed in Europe.[15] In the words of Bernard Drachman, Lieberman was "a thoroughly cultured gentleman entirely abreast of the scientific thought of the age, a masterly Talmudist and a sturdy consistent Israelite."[16] In the early years of the Seminary, Drachman and Lieberman were the only paid members of the faculty, serving, respectively, as Professors of Bible and Talmud; and the students would also hear lectures by members of the Advisory Board, as well as Cyrus Adler.

From its original Preparatory Class of eight students, the Seminary grew steadily. As we have seen, in its second academic

---

[13]Ibid., August 19, 1887, p. 21.

[14]S. Morais, sermon, "On the Opening of a Higher Class at the J.T. Seminary," Dec. 1887, Morais Papers.

[15]Drachman, *Light*, p. 183.

[16]Letter from B. Drachman to S. Morais, Oct. 28, 1887, quoted in Nussenbaum, *Champion*, p. 122.

year, there were 19 students; and, by the fall of 1889, there were 25 students.[17] The 1890 *Proceedings* of the Seminary Association lists only 13 students;[18] and the discrepancy of numbers probably derives from the fact that the Seminary generally had a large number of individuals auditing courses who were not officially enrolled until they displayed an adequate knowledge of the English language. In 1892, when the Seminary opened its first Senior Class, there were 16 students formally enrolled; and by 1894, there were 26. For the next eight years, until the reorganization of the Seminary, the number of students remained approximately the same, reaching a high point of 32 in 1898,[19] and levelling off to 27 in 1900. By comparison, the Hebrew Union College had 37 students in 1886, and 73 by 1900.[20] Although most of the students in the Seminary's first class did not complete their studies, by the mid-1890's, the great majority of them went on to ordination. By this time the average Seminary student was in his early twenties and attended the institution so as to fulfill definite career goals.

One of the interesting aspects of the early Seminary student enrollment is the fact that from approximately 1892 to 1896, Sabato Morais taught two young men privately in Philadelphia—Gerson Levi and Isaac Husik.[21] These young scholars were formally enrolled in the Seminary, despite the fact that all of their studies took place in Philadelphia. The idea was that after completing most of their studies with Dr. Morais, they would join the Senior Class in New York. Gerson Levi did, indeed, proceed to graduate from the Seminary in the time of Solomon Schechter; but Isaac Husik never attended the New York school, graduating instead from the University of Pennsylvania, after which he went on to a distinguished career as a scholar of medieval Jewish philosophy.

In order to gain admission to the Seminary, a young man had to submit an application, signed by his parents, in which he stated whether he wished "to become a teacher, rabbi, or reader," and certified to "his adherence to the mode of life consonant with Jewish

[17]*AH*, Oct. 25, 1889, cover page.
[18]*Proceedings*, J.T.S.A., 1890, p. 66.
[19]*Proceedings*, J.T.S.A., 1898, p. 7.
[20]*American Israelite*, Nov. 19, 1886, p. 4; Meyer, "Centennial History," p. 46.
[21]*Proceedings*, J.T.S.A., 1892, p. 28; 1894, p. 27; 1896, p. 28.

Laws."[22] After submitting his application to the "Seminary Committee," as it was called, the candidate would then be examined by members of the Advisory Board, especially Dr. Morais, in order to ascertain the depth of his Jewish knowledge. In order to be admitted to the Preparatory Department, a student had to "be able to translate easy passages in the Bible and Talmud, possess some knowledge of Jewish history and be able to speak the English language."[23] Since many of the students were born in Europe, they often applied with a more extensive Jewish knowledge; and students with advanced standing were admitted to higher classes. In 1890, the trustees decided that, "No student over twenty-one years of age shall be admitted unless qualified to enter college; nor any over twenty-five years of age, unless possessed of secular education equivalent to the requirement for the degree of Bachelor of Arts."[24] Indeed, from the very beginning, the leaders of the Seminary felt that a college education was vital for its graduates, so as to enable them to represent the very best of secular, as well as Jewish, culture; and in 1896, the trustees formally agreed with the recommendation of Dr. Morais that no student should be ordained unless he had first received a college or university degree.[25]

The earliest students of the Seminary were quite young—in their early teens—and the professors were plagued by both behavior and attendance problems. Writing to Morais in June, 1888, Pereira Mendes reported on a meeting that he had held with Joseph Blumenthal and Dr. Drachman: "Many things must be changed in our regime, and while I have no time now to enter into details I will say that we must mix Draco with Solon."[26] As late as 1894, reporting on the progress of the Senior Class, Morais lamented to the trustees, "I regret, however, that the Cuzari, which ought to have commanded the profound reflection of our students, was abandoned by reason of insufficient regularity in the attendance, on the part of the instructed."[27] While behavior problems ceased in the

---

[22]*Proceedings*, J.T.S.A., 1890, p. 50.
[23]*AH*, August 31, 1888, p. 8.
[24]*Proceedings*, J.T.S.A., 1890, p. 50.
[25]*Proceedings*, J.T.S.A., 1896, p. 36.
[26]Letter from H.P. Mendes to S. Morais, June 18, 1888, Morais Papers.
[27]*Proceedings*, J.T.S.A., 1894, p. 26.

1890's, as the age of the average student increased, attendance was a recurrent problem, principally because the students were busy much of the day with their secular university studies, and often did not find the time to complete their work at the Seminary.

Another interesting problem which arose in the early years concerned the religious policy of the Seminary with respect to the part-time pulpits which the students often assumed in order to support themselves and to develop their rabbinic skills. In June, 1888, Pereira Mendes wrote to Morais concerning such a problem:

> Our student Friedlander lectured at a Synagogue in Brooklyn, representing that it was orthodox. But it appears that they have recently tolerated the pew system. Personally he is opposed. They have now elected him their minister. I told him he would either have to quit the Seminary or submit to our directions. He has therefore written to the president accordingly, and will refuse the position unless the pew matter can be adjusted. But he says he is in great want; he gets but ten dollars a month, has lost his lesson by which he earned somewhat, (for people stop study in summer) needs more than our stipend of ten dollars to live, even most moderately, and is at a loss to buy books. I gave him a couple of dollars yesterday, do you not think we should do something for him over the summer if he cannot get the position in Brooklyn?[28]

The congregation apparently complied with the wishes of the Seminary, for, one month later, the *American Hebrew* noted that Mr. Friedlander had assumed the pulpit of Congregation Beth Israel in Brooklyn.[29]

Pereira Mendes's letter refers poignantly to the poverty that most of the early Seminary students had to endure. As Dr. Morais noted in a sermon in December, 1887, "it is, as a rule, the poor that will devote their best years to qualify themselves for the pulpit."[30] The reasons that the sons of the wealthy did not pursue rabbinical studies were that, in the 1880's and 1890's, the rabbinate was only

---

[28]Letter from H.P. Mendes to S. Morais, June 18, 1888, Morais Papers.

[29]*AH*, July 27, 1888, p. 8.

[30]S. Morais, sermon, "On the Opening of a Higher Class at the J.T. Seminary," Dec. 1887, Morais Papers.

just beginning to acquire the status of a profession, most rabbis were still poorly paid, and the wealthy generally preferred their sons to enter commerce or more lucrative professions such as law or medicine. Most of the Seminary students came from the ghetto of the Lower East Side; and the institution not only had to provide them with a small financial stipend, it often gave them clothes as well, provided freely by a member of the Board of Trustees, S.W. Korn, who was in the clothing business, as well as by other local friends. Interestingly, the early Hebrew Union College also had to supply free clothing to its students; and, again like the Seminary, it had to provide financial aid to most of its young scholars.[31]

In determining the curriculum and the educational philosophy of the early Seminary, the basic model was the Jewish Theological Seminary of Breslau, in Germany, which had been organized in 1854 under the leadership of Rabbi Zacharias Frankel.[32] Enunciating a philosophy of "positive historical Judaism," Frankel combined a moderate acceptance of religious reforms, along with an essential traditionalism, to fashion a theology which is often seen as the spiritual ancestor of contemporary Conservative Judaism.[33] Although Morais did consult with the leaders of Jews' College in London before planning the Seminary's curriculum,[34] there is little doubt that the Breslau school provided the primary model for the instruction in New York. Alexander Kohut, who, along with Morais, helped to fashion the Seminary's curriculum and later taught at the institution, was a graduate of Breslau, as was Rabbi Frederick de Sola Mendes of the Advisory Board. Perhaps most importantly, Bernard Drachman, who provided a great deal of the day-to-day instruction at the Seminary, was a Breslau graduate as well. The Breslau Seminary offered a seven-year program leading to ordination, which stressed not only Talmud and Codes, but also

[31]Meyer, "Centennial History," p. 26.

[32]Davis, *Yahadut Amerika*, p. 258.

[33]See Ismar Schorsch, "Zacharias Frankel and the European Origins of Conservative Judaism," in *Judaism*, Vol. 30, No. 3 (Summer, 1981), pp. 344-354; also Herbert Rosenblum, *Conservative Judaism: A Contemporary History* (N.Y., 1983) p. 78.

[34]Nussenbaum, *Champion*, p. 119.

Bible, Jewish history, philosophy, Midrash, and homiletics—the very same program that the New York Seminary later presented.[35]

The curriculum of the early Seminary was a valiant attempt to familiarize the students with a broad spectrum of Jewish knowledge. Whereas the traditional Eastern European *yeshiva* confined its instruction largely to Talmud and Codes, the Seminary stressed not only these subjects but also Bible, Midrash, Hebrew language, Jewish history, philosophy, and "practical rabbinics." Indeed, with the exception of Pastoral Psychology and Modern Hebrew Literature, the early Seminary students pursued a course of study that is remarkably similar to that which is offered one hundred years later—a great testimony to the wisdom of the founders, who wished to establish the Seminary as a first-rate academic institution from its very beginning. The course of study was envisioned as nine years, but many students entered the school with more than an elementary background from Europe, and were immediately placed in a higher grade.

In 1890, the Seminary Association *Proceedings* set forth the model curriculum for the new institution:[36]

Preparatory Department

1st Year: Genesis 12-50 and Exodus with Rashi and Hebrew
Grammar, 2 hours a week
Samuel and Kings at sight, 2 hours
History to Solomon, 1 hour
Psalm Translation, 1 hour

2nd Year: Leviticus and Numbers with Rashi and Grammar,
2 hours a week
Joshua and Judges at sight, 1 hour
Mishnah: Berachot and Shabat, 2 hours
History to Ezra, 1 hour

---

[35]Drachman, *Light*, pp. 99-109.
[36]*Proceedings*, J.T.S.A., 1890, pp. 52-54.

3rd Year: Deuteronomy with Rashi, 1 hour a week
Jeremiah and Lamentations, Nehemiah, 2 hours
Mishnah: Pesachim and Yoma, 2 hours
Aramaic portions of the Bible with grammar, 1 hour
History to destruction of the 2nd Temple, 1 hour

Junior Department

1st Year: Torah with commentary and Onkelos,
2 hours a week
Isaiah with commentary, 2 hours
Talmud: Berachot and Pesahim with Rashi, 4 hours
Hebrew Prose Composition
History to Amoraim, 1 hour
Essays on Jewish History
Voluntary instruction in *hazzanut*

2nd Year: Hosea with commentaries, 2 hours
Avot with commentaries, text memorized, 2 hours
Talmud: Shabat with commentary, 2 hours
Rosh Hashana at sight, 2 hours
Hebrew Prose Composition
History to Geonim, 1 hour
Essays on Jewish History
Lectures on Homiletics and Pedagogy—history and
methods, 1 hour (lst term)
Lectures on Biblical Archaeology (2nd term)
Voluntary instruction in *hazzanut*

Senior Department

1st Year: Bible: Psalms with ancient and modern commen-
taries, 2 hours a week
(2nd term)
Ezekiel with commentaries, 2 hours (lst term)
Lectures on History of Biblical Exegesis and
Versions, 1 hour
Midrash Raba, 2 hours

Talmud: Gittin with commentaries, Avodah Zarah at
    sight, 2 hours *each*
Jewish Philosophy: Selections from R. Joseph Albo's
    Sefer HaIkarim, 2 hours
History from Geon R. Channa to R. Shmuel
    HaNagid, 1 hour
Hebrew Composition
English Essays: Jewish Religion and Philosophy
Practice in conducting services and teaching
General Survey of Semitic Languages, 1 hour
    (2nd term)
Course for teachers and *Hazzanim* ends with this
    grade.

2nd Year: Lectures on History of Biblical Versions, 1 hour
Job with commentary, 1 hour
Midrash, 2 hours
Talmud: Hullin with commentary, 4 hours
    Sanhedrin at sight, 2 hours
    Poskim, Orach Hayyim, 1 hour
Homiletics, 1 hour
Philosophy, *Emunot V'Deot*, 2 hours
Lectures on History of Jewish Philosophy, 1 hour
Hebrew and English Composition (on History of
    Jewish Literature)
History to death of Maimonides, 1 hour

3rd Year: Minor Prophets with commentaries, ancient and
    modern, 2 hours a week
Talmud: Hullin, 6 hours
    Baba Metzia at sight, 2 hours
    Kiddushin thoroughly, 4 hours
Poskim, Yoreh Deah, Even HaEzer, selections,
    2 hours
Moreh Nebuchim, selections, 2 hours
Selected Responsa, 2 hours
History to Modern Times, 1 hour

Essays on Biblical and Talmudical themes
Homiletical Exercises

4th Year: Talmud: Hullin, 6 hours
Yevamot, Ch. 10, 4 hours
Yoma at sight, 2 hours
Sukkah, 2 hours
Talmud Yerushalmi, 2 hours
Philosophy: Kuzari, 2 hours
Responsa, 2 hours
Yoreh Deah, 3 hours
Midrash, 3 hours
Practice of Homiletics in English and German
Essays on Biblical and Talmudical themes
Lectures: General Survey of the Talmud, 1 hour
(1st term)
General Survey of Oriental History, 1 hour
(2nd term)

Although this curriculum was an ambitious one, to an extraordinary degree the students completed most of the work that the founders envisioned, with the exception that the Talmud load had to be lightened somewhat. Perhaps the only major change that was made in the implementation of this curriculum was the fact that the early Seminary could not conceivably offer nine different course levels, given the small faculty and the limited funds at the institution's disposal. Instead, the classes were generally combined so as to form two classes of Seniors, two classes of Juniors, and two classes of Preparatory students.

As an example of how much was actually studied at the Seminary, we have the 1900 instructors' reports to the trustees of Dr. Drachman and Professor Joshua Joffe, who succeeded Dr. Lieberman in 1893. In the two academic years from 1898 to 1900, under the tutelage of Professor Joffe, the Senior A and Graduating Classes studied 178 pages of Gemara Ketubot, with commentary, as well as ample selections from the Yerushalmi, Mishneh Torah, and other Rabbinic works. With Dr. Drachman, they covered the Minor Prophets, almost all of the *Kuzari* of Rabbi Yehuda Halevy, and studied Jewish History and History of Exegesis as well.[37] Although the reports do not mention "practical" courses, such as homiletics, the older students most surely studied pulpit skills, being required to preach regularly in the Seminary Synagogue on Shabat afternoons. A similar comparison of the lower classes with the theoretical curriculum outlined in the *Proceedings* yields the same result—that the reality generally lived up to the high goals set by the founders.

The curriculum of the early Seminary was based upon that of the Jewish Theological Seminary of Breslau. In both schools Bible and exegesis played a key role in the curriculum, along with Talmud and Codes; and interestingly, both schools presented a course in Biblical Archaeology. Other subjects presented at both institutions were Jewish History, Philosophy, Midrash, Homiletics, and Hebrew Grammar. Nevertheless, there were some differences between the programs as well. In New York, the students had an opportunity to study *hazzanut*; whereas in Breslau, the curriculum included courses in Pedagogy and in the intricacies of the Jewish calendar.[38] The curriculum of the Seminary was also very similar to that of the Hebrew Union College, except that the Cincinnati school also offered courses in "Semitics," teaching languages such as Syriac and Arabic. The J.T.S. senior students apparently studied more Talmud, but the H.U.C. students were required to write a thesis before ordination, which was not required at the Seminary.[39]

With such a demanding curriculum at the Seminary, the students were often hard-pressed to complete both their secular and religious studies. In 1894, for a very brief period, the Seminary tried a radical solution to this vexing dilemma. In his 1894 report to the Seminary Association Convention, President Joseph Blumenthal revealed a new development at the Seminary:

> Various circumstances operated to hinder the progress of several pupils in the College of the City of New York, where the demands of the curriculum, particularly in the mathematical branches, were of an

---

[37]*Proceedings*, J.T.S.A., 1900, pp. 17-18.

[38]M. Brann, *Geschichte des Jüdisch-Theologischen Seminars (Fraenckel'sche Stiftung) in Breslau* (Breslau, 1904), p. 68.

[39]Meyer, "Centennial History," pp. 21-22.

inordinately burdensome character. We have, therefore, been
compelled to establish an academic department, with two competent
instructors, and six students are now pursuing their secular studies in
this department, which includes instruction in Latin, Greek, German,
history, English Literature, algebra, geometry, physics, and advanced
English.[40]

Curiously, there is no other record of this secular studies department at the Seminary. It could not have lasted very long, for at the
1896 Convention, Blumenthal once again lamented that a solution
had not yet been devised so as "to accommodate the severe demands upon the time of our students made by the pursuit of secular
studies in college, with the necessity for doing full justice to the requirements of our curriculum and schedule of studies here in the
Seminary."[41] There is no mention of a secular studies department in
the 1896 *Proceedings*; and not one word about this department was
ever printed in the *American Hebrew*, which generally gave a running account of all the activities and developments at the Seminary.

The key to the implementation of the Seminary's curriculum
was, of course, the faculty; and the mainstay of the faculty was
Bernard Drachman, who taught at the institution all the way down
to 1909, when he was dismissed after an apparent dispute with
Solomon Schechter.[42] Although Drachman came to represent the
"orthodox" point of view on the Schechter faculty, and later taught
for many years at the Rabbi Isaac Elchanan Theological Seminary,
the truth is that when he first came to the Seminary, he served in a
congregation with mixed seating,[43] and very definitely represented
the point of view of the "Historical School."[44] With a B.A. and an
M.A. from Columbia University, a Ph.D. from the University of
Heidelberg, as well as rabbinical ordination from Dr. M. Joel of
Breslau, Drachman was an articulate and highly competent instruc-

[40]*Proceedings*, J.T.S.A ., 1894, p. 16.

[41]*Proceedings*, J.T.S.A., 1896, p. 17.

[42]Drachman, *Light*, pp. 259-260.

[43]Ibid., p. 185.

[44]See *AH*, Nov. 15, 1895, pp. 42-43, for Drachman's defense of "Historical or
Orthodox Judaism."

tor, whose ongoing presence, both as professor and as dean, provided a much-needed sense of continuity in the early Seminary.

Joining the faculty towards the end of 1887, Dr. Gustave Lieberman was the Seminary's first Talmud professor. When Dr. Lieberman left the Seminary after approximately five years to become the administrator of the Bronx Lebanon Hospital, he was succeeded by Professor Joshua A. Joffe, who remained at the institution all the way down to 1917. Born in Minsk, Russia, in 1862, Professor Joffe had studied in the famous Yeshiva of Volozhin and had received his *semicha* from Rabbi I.J. Reines in 1881 and from the Berlin Hochschule in 1888. His ordination from the Reform-leaning Hochschule demonstrates that Joffe, much like Solomon Schechter, was an individual who had consciously rejected the rigidity of Eastern European orthodoxy; and in this sense, his background was very different from the Western European training of other Seminary leaders such as Drachman, Morais, and Pereira Mendes. In addition to holding several rabbinic positions in Europe, Joffe also studied Semitics, History, and Philosophy (with Moritz Lazarus) at the University of Berlin, and came to the United States in 1892.[45] While serving as Professor of Talmud, Joffe also took a great interest in the extracurricular activities of the students, helping them to develop a fluency in the Hebrew language, and taking an active role in the students' Literary Society.

In addition to the two "major" professorships at the Seminary, both of which were paid positions, the institution also utilized the services of numerous other individuals, on a part-time basis. First and foremost, there was Sabato Morais, the beloved rabbi, who even in his seventies would make the arduous train trip from Philadelphia three times a week in order to supervise the school, which he often referred to as his "Benjamin"— the child of his old age. As President of the Faculty, totally unpaid, Morais took a deep, personal interest in each and every one of the students, winning their love and affection.[46] In addition to his administrative duties, which involved interviewing each prospective student and faculty

---

[45]*AJYB*, 1904-1905, p. 125.

[46]Joseph Elmaleh recalls how even in advanced years, his father, Leon, would always speak about Dr. Morais with profound respect and awe. (Interview, Dec. 26, 1983.)

member, Morais would lecture from time to time on the Bible or on some aspect of Jewish theology.

In 1892, Morais became quite ill, and upon his recovery, the trustees attempted to persuade him to remain in New York on a permanent basis, so as to give more direction to the school. Henry Pereira Mendes even volunteered to resign his position as first minister of Shearith Israel, and to serve as Morais's assistant, in order to get him to accept the trustees' offer. Nevertheless, flattered as he was by these offers, Morais declined to accept the proposal out of loyalty to Mikveh Israel, declaring, "I could never entertain it. To tear myself away from Philadelphia would be to tear the very fibres of my heart."[47]

On his seventieth birthday, in 1893, the students made a gala celebration for Dr. Morais; and in his honor, the trustees named the Seminary Library after him.[48] Four years later, the Seminary once again celebrated Dr. Morais's birthday, as the students and the trustees presented him with a magnificent portrait as a birthday gift.[49] When Dr. Morais died in November, 1897, his passing was an irreparable loss for the Seminary, not only because of his academic competence, but also because of his passionate devotion and dedication to the institution. As the leading traditional rabbi in America, Morais had lent tremendous prestige to the Seminary; and, as we shall see, his passing made it imperative to find a new leader who would command the respect of all American Jews.

In addition to Dr. Morais, the Seminary was also blessed in its early years with the voluntary services of Dr. Alexander Kohut, who was a first-rate scholar. Despite the fact that he was a busy congregational rabbi and deeply involved in his own scholarly pursuits, Kohut still managed to teach at the Seminary on a part-time basis for a number of years. In 1890, Kohut became "Professor of Midrashic Literature" at the Seminary, and he later taught a course in the "Methodology of the Talmud."[50] In his study of Rabbinic literature, Kohut was, in the modern sense, a critical scholar; but like

---

[47]Sabato Morais, untitled sermon on his 41st anniversary in the Jewish Ministry, c. 1892, Morais Papers.

[48]*AH*, April 21, 1893, pp. 802-803, 823.

[49]Ibid., May 7, 1897, p. 12.

[50]*Proceedings*, J.T.S.A., 1894, p. 28.

Dr. Morais, he refused to apply his critical techniques to the words of the Torah: "The sooner we turn away from the Kuenen Wellhausen hypercritical absurdities the better we will be off [sic] in an unbiased investigation of Holy Scriptures . . . To us the Pentateuch is a *noli me tangere!* Hands off!"[51] While there is no doubt that Dr. Kohut was truthful in his views on the Torah, it should be noted that if he had openly held any other position, he most likely would not have been permitted to teach at the Seminary for fear of further eroding the orthodox support for the institution. Like Morais, Dr. Kohut won the deep admiration and respect of his students; and even though his last year was filled with illness, he continued to teach his Seminary pupils from his bedside. When he died in May, 1894, the Seminary lost the most prestigious scholar it was to have on the faculty until the arrival of Solomon Schechter.

Another member of the Advisory Board who taught at the Seminary was Henry Pereira Mendes, who served part-time as Professor of Jewish History. As minister of New York's most prestigious traditional synagogue, Shearith Israel, the presence of Mendes on the faculty lent stature to the institution despite the fact that he did not have outstanding scholarly credentials. After the passing of Morais, Mendes assumed the title of Acting President of the Faculty, a position he consented to accept until a full-time president could be found. Serving voluntarily as part-time Professor of Shulchan Aruch from approximately 1894 to 1902 was Rabbi Moses Maisner of Congregation Adath Israel in New York. A native of Hungary, Maisner had received a Ph.D. from the University of Pest, and had been ordained by the distinguished Rabbi A.S.B.W. Sofer of Pressburg.[52] Another part-time professor, from the earliest days of the Seminary, was Cyrus Adler, who taught Biblical Archaeology. Although Adler worked in Washington at the Smithsonian Institution and could only teach sporadically at the Seminary, all of the school's publications proudly proclaimed him as a member of the faculty. The reason for this is very simple: as a native-born American with a Ph.D. from Johns Hopkins, and as a distinguished member of the Smithsonian staff, Adler's name would certainly add

---

[51]*AH*, July 1, 1892, p. 279.
[52]*AJYB*, 1903-1904, p. 77.

great prestige to the Seminary. In addition, the Seminary leaders were eager to refute the canard that traditional Judaism is backward or old-fashioned, and having a professor of Biblical Archaeology on the faculty could only serve to enhance the image of the institution.

Rounding out the list of Advisory Board members who also served as part-time professors is Rabbi David Davidson, the successor to Alexander Kohut at Congregation Ahavath Chesed. Born in Germany in 1848, Davidson studied with Zacharias Frankel in Breslau, came to America in 1880, and served as rabbi in Des Moines and Cincinnati. While in Cincinnati, Davidson served as a Professor of Biblical Literature and Talmud at the Hebrew Union College from 1885 to 1892, and also became a member of the Central Conference of American Rabbis, an organization of Reform rabbis.[53] After serving as rabbi in Montgomery, Alabama for three years, Davidson came to New York in 1895 to succeed Dr. Kohut. Not only was Rabbi Davidson named to the Advisory Board, he also served as Professor of "Rabbinica" at the Seminary from 1896 to 1902. Although, at first glance, it appears surprising that the Seminary would utilize the services of an individual who not only had taught at the Hebrew Union College, but was also a highly regarded member of the C.C.A.R.,[54] a number of factors should be kept in mind. First, Ahavath Chesed was a substantial supporter of the Seminary, and it would have been unwise for the Seminary leaders to snub the rabbi of this congregation by not appointing him to the Advisory Board or asking him to teach. Second, although Ahavath Chesed was a moderate Reform congregation, in which *taleisim* were not even worn, Rabbi Davidson, like Dr. Kohut, appears to have had strong traditionalist leanings. Finally, the Seminary seems to have had great difficulty finding professors who could teach Talmud in English;[55] and with his previous teaching experience at the Hebrew Union College, Davidson was a logical choice to serve on the Seminary faculty.

---

[53]*American Israelite*, July 16, 1886, p. 5; also *Universal Jewish Encyclopedia* (N.Y., 1941), vol. 3, p. 488.

[54]Rabbi Davidson delivered the opening prayer at the C.C.A.R. convention in Montreal in 1897; see *AH*, June 9, 1897, p. 307.

[55]Gilbert Klaperman, *The Story of Yeshiva University: The First Jewish University in America* (no location given, 1969), p. 41.

In addition to the individuals who held professorial rank, there were several other men who were designated as "preceptors" and who taught for generally short periods of time at the Seminary. One such instructor was Rev. Pinchos Minkowsky, who is mentioned in the 1890 *Proceedings* as teaching *hazzanut*.[56] Although Minkowsky's tenure at the Seminary was probably very brief, for he is not mentioned in any other extant Seminary source, it is interesting to note that he was one of the most famous cantors in the world of his time, who had been lured from his native Russia to the Eldridge Street Congregation in New York by an offer of the princely sum of $5,000 for himself and his choir.[57] The presence of such a distinguished individual on the Seminary faculty, even in an extremely limited role, could only serve to increase the prestige of the institution in the eyes of the community.

The teaching of *hazzanut* was sporadic at best in the early Seminary; for although various cantors would offer lessons from time to time, the 1892 *Proceedings* notes that this "desirable instruction has unavoidably been abandoned, for want of a person who can find the leisure to impart it."[58] Although various members of the Advisory Board and others may have offered some instruction in liturgy thereafter, the only formal mention of a faculty member for *hazzanut* after that time is found in the 1900 *Proceedings* where Rev. S. Jacobson is listed as preceptor of "Ritual and Liturgy."[59]

Ever eager to improve the students' speaking skills, the Seminary not only provided regular instruction and practice in homiletics, it also employed a special professor just to teach the art of elocution. In 1892, Professor Robert Houston of City College was engaged to teach this subject;[60] and the position was later held by Professor Henry S. Carr and Montague Lessler. Although it might seem unusual for the Seminary to employ teachers who were probably not Jewish, the subject was most likely taught in a totally secu-

---

[56]*Proceedings*, J.T.S.A., 1890, p. 11.

[57]Macy Nulman, *Concise Encyclopedia of Jewish Music* (N.Y., 1975), p. 174; Eisenstein, "History," pp. 150-151.

[58]*Proceedings*, J.T.S.A., 1892, p. 29.

[59]*Proceedings*, J.T.S.A., 1900, p. 5.

[60]*AH*, Jan. 29, 1892, p. 262.

lar fashion; and no objections to their employment seem to have
been raised. Sabato Morais took a special interest in the study of the
Hebrew language; and so it is not surprising that from approximately 1895 to 1900, the Seminary employed Moses Khazon, a well-
known local Hebraist, to teach Hebrew Composition.[61] We have
already mentioned that the Seminary had considerable difficulty
finding instructors who were capable of teaching in English, and it
is possibly for this reason that, from 1892 to 1895, it employed a
gifted Senior student, Henry M. Speaker, to teach Bible and Talmud
to the Preparatory classes. After his ordination in 1895, Speaker
continued to teach at the Seminary for another two years; and upon
his leaving to become principal of Gratz College in 1897, his position
was taken over by another learned Senior student, Solomon Reich,[62]
who was, in turn, succeeded by Max Switton in 1899-1900.[63]

Thus, from the original faculty which consisted of only Dr.
Drachman and the part-time instructors of the Advisory Board, the
Seminary teaching staff came to include ten men by 1900, six of
whom were paid. By comparison, although the Hebrew Union
College had more than twice as many students as the Seminary by
1900, it employed the same number of faculty members.[64] The
image and prestige of the Seminary also grew from its early years;
and in 1892, the trustees rejoiced when President Seth Low and the
trustees of Columbia University placed J.T.S. "in the same relation
to the College [Columbia] which is borne by the Union Theological
Seminary and the General Theological Seminary"—namely that its
students who qualified for admission to Columbia could attend on a
tuition-free basis.[65]

As the Seminary faculty and student enrollment grew, the institution grew physically as well. The Seminary began its life in the
vestry room of Congregation Shearith Israel on West 19th Street; but
this arrangement soon proved unsatisfactory, and in October, 1887,
it moved to the Cooper Union building on 8th Street and Fourth
Avenue, where it rented rooms for four years. In September, 1891,

---

[61]*Proceedings*, J.T.S.A., 1896, p. 6.
[62]*Proceedings*, J.T.S.A., 1898, pp. 14, 25.
[63]*Proceedings*, J.T.S.A., 1900, p. 17.
[64]Meyer, "Centennial History," p. 46.
[65]*Proceedings*, J.T.S.A., 1892, p. 16.

the Seminary moved to a large apartment at 220 East 12th Street;[66] but the need for larger and more substantial quarters was apparent to all. Finally, in the spring of 1892, the Seminary acquired its first building—a large brownstone house at 736 Lexington Avenue, near 59th Street. With five floors, the building contained space for "three classrooms, a large library and reading room, a lecture hall, reception room [which was used as a synagogue], janitor's quarters, and an entire floor for dormitories."[67] The total cost of the building was $19,500; and after a down payment of $7,500, which included a gift of $3,000 from Jacob Schiff, the mortgage was $12,000.[68]

On May 25, 1892, the Seminary's first building was dedicated with gala ceremonies, and an honored guest at the program was Seth Low, the president of Columbia University. The dormitory facilities of the building proved especially useful, for, by 1896, they housed eleven students, most of whom were from New York, but who found it easier to live there than to commute. Although Lexington Avenue was at that time a rapidly growing Jewish area, a place of "second settlement" after the Lower East Side,[69] the new facilities proved to be unsatisfactory. Thus, in 1898, just six years after the Seminary moved to its new home, the Advisory Board made this recommendation to the Convention of the Seminary Association:

> We take this opportunity of expressing our hope that at an early date the Seminary will be moved to more academic surroundings. Its present location in a busy and somewhat noisy neighborhood, is very objectionable, as undisturbed quiet is absolutely necessary for study and for teaching.[70]

Within a few years, the Advisory Board members got their wish, for shortly after the arrival of Solomon Schechter, through the gen-

---

[66]*AH*, Sept. 19, 1891, p, 164.

[67]Ibid., May 20, 1892, p. 84.

[68]Ibid., March 17, 1893, p. 651; *Proceedings*, J.T.S.A., 1894, p. 12.

[69]Moses Rischin,*The Promised City: New York's Jews 1870-1914* (N.Y., 1970), p. 93.

[70]*Proceedings*, J.T.S.A., 1898, p. 26.

erosity of Jacob Schiff, a new home was constructed for the institution on West 123rd Street, across the street from its present location.

The Seminary library also grew rapidly in its early years. Starting with small gifts from Sabato Morais, Cyrus Adler, and others, the Seminary acquired part of the library of Rabbi A.S. Bettelheim of Baltimore in 1890, as a donation from his son-in-law, Alexander Kohut; and the institution later acquired the rest of this collection from Mrs. Bettelheim in 1893. To honor Dr. Morais on his seventieth birthday in April, 1893, the Seminary trustees named the library after him; and Professor Joshua Joffe was selected to serve as librarian. At that time, the Seminary library only consisted of about 1,000 volumes; but shortly thereafter the Morais Library expanded tremendously when the private collection of Dr. David Cassel of Berlin was obtained, adding another 3,000 volumes.[71] Active in the *Wissenschaft* movement, Cassel was a distinguished scholar and professor at the Berlin Hochschule, and his library certainly represented a very valuable acquisition for the Seminary.

In the following months and years, gifts of books were received from many individuals, most notably Marx and Moses Ottinger, Alexander Kohut, Mrs. Henry S. Jacobs, and David Sulzberger of Philadelphia. From Lemberg, the great Rabbinic scholar, Solomon Buber, sent a thirteen-volume collection of his own works; and from St. Petersburg, Professor Alexander Harkavy also sent one of his works.[72] In June, 1894, Sabato Morais presented the Library with 500 selected volumes; and, upon his passing, he willed all the remainder of his Hebrew books to the Seminary, adding another 700 volumes. While we have no exact figure, by 1900, the Seminary Library must have encompassed at least 6,000 volumes—a good start, but still small in comparison to the more than 13,000 volumes owned by the Hebrew Union College.[73]

So far, we have discussed the actual growth of the Seminary in terms of its students, faculty, curriculum, and physical facilities; but the highlight of the Seminary's early existence was its first graduation, in June, 1894. After an all-day examination in every aspect of

---

[71]Solis Cohen, "J.T.S. Past and Future," p. 28.

[72]*Proceedings*, J.T.S.A., 1894, pp. 21-22.

[73]*AH*, Dec. 24, 1896, p. 227.

Jewish lore, conducted by a panel of local rabbis, three students were deemed worthy to stand forth as the first products of the Seminary—Joseph Hertz as rabbi, and David Wittenberg and Henry M. Speaker as teachers. Hertz was a brilliant young man who had received his B.A. from City College in 1891, winning the Riggs Medal for scholarship, and who received his Ph.D. from Columbia the day before his ordination from the Seminary. On the Sabbath before the graduation ceremonies, Rev. Henry Pereira Mendes delivered the baccalaureate sermon in Shearith Israel, proudly proclaiming that, "for the first time in the history of American Judaism, a graduate trained with an eight years' course, is sent forth—trained in the Seminary of the Historical School of Judaism, trained in Hebrew study, trained to love, to revere, to practice the Law of Moses and to respect the admonitions of our sages."[74]

Finally, on Thursday evening, June 14, 1894, at Carnegie Chamber Music Hall in Manhattan, the great event took place. After opening remarks by President Blumenthal, Rev. Pereira Mendes offered a prayer for the graduates, and then Dr. Morais gave a charge to each of the young men. Mr. Blumenthal then called the graduates to the platform, and presented the Teachers' Certificates to Speaker and Wittenberg, after which Dr. Drachman "read the Hattarath Horaiah" to Joseph Hertz, who received diplomas in both Hebrew and English.[75] Called upon to deliver the valedictory, Rabbi Hertz gave a stirring address in support of traditional Judaism and in praise of Drs. Kohut and Morais; and he declared that Seminary-trained rabbis "must become the determined enemy of all flippancy, of all irreverent sneering at divine things—the sin of American Jewish life."[76]

The festivities surrounding the ordination of Joseph Hertz did not end with the conclusion of the graduation ceremony. The next morning, Rabbi Hertz and his father, Joseph Blumenthal, Max Cohen, and Revs. H.P. Mendes and Bernard Drachman all took the train to Syracuse, where Hertz was to be installed as rabbi of Congregation Adath Jeshurun. After an entire weekend of banquet-

---

[74]Ibid., June 15, 1894, p. 209.
[75]Ibid., June 22, 1894, p. 242.
[76]Ibid., June 22, 1894, p. 243.

ing and speeches, Rabbi Hertz was formally installed in his new position; and, to honor the event, a Syracuse Branch of the Seminary Association was founded.[77]

The following year, in September, 1895, David Wittenberg and Henry M. Speaker were ordained as rabbis and Emil Friedman graduated as a *hazzan* and teacher. Speaker continued to serve as an instructor at the Seminary, and became chaplain at Sing Sing Prison. Wittenberg became rabbi of Congregation Beth El in Buffalo; and, once again, a Seminary delegation accompanied him to his new congregation, and a Buffalo Branch of the Seminary Association was founded.[78] Friedman continued to serve in the cantorial position he had held as a student, serving as *hazzan* of Congregation Adath Israel on 125th Street in Manhattan. In the sixteen years from its foundation to its reorganization, the Jewish Theological Seminary graduated the following seventeen men, fourteen as rabbis, and three as *hazzanim*:

1894	Joseph H. Hertz
1895	Emil Friedman (*hazzan*)
	Henry Speaker
	David Wittenberg
1898	Bernard M. Kaplan
	Morris Mandel
1899	Menahem M. Eichler
	Leon H. Elmaleh (*hazzan*)
	Michael Fried
1900	Julius H. Greenstone
	David Levine
1902	Herman Abramowitz
	Aaron P. Drucker
	Israel Goldfarb (*hazzan*)
	Phineas Israeli
	Mordecai M. Kaplan
	Charles H. Kauvar

[77]*Proceedings*, J.T.S.A., 1896, pp. 12-13.
[78]*AH*, Oct. 25, 1895, p. 636.

In addition, in 1902, the Seminary awarded the title of "Preacher and Teacher" to Nathan Wolf and Alter Abelson.[79]

Several of these men went on to careers of great distinction in the Jewish world. Joseph Hertz held pulpits in Syracuse, Johannesburg, and New York, before becoming Chief Rabbi of the British Commonwealth in 1913. A distinguished scholar and Biblical commentator, Hertz was the editor of a well-known commentary on the Pentateuch which is still in use in many traditional English-speaking synagogues. Mordecai M. Kaplan served on the Seminary faculty for many years and was the founding dean of the Teachers' Institute. A profound theologian and writer, Kaplan is generally regarded as the founder of the Reconstructionist Movement. Henry M. Speaker was the founding principal of Gratz College, and served in that capacity for over thirty years. Julius H. Greenstone also taught at Gratz College for many decades and served as principal there from 1933 to 1948. Author of *The Religion of Israel* and *The Jewish Religion*, as well as of commentaries on Numbers and Proverbs that were published by the Jewish Publication Society, "Greenstone was among the first American Jews to produce books of popular Jewish scholarship in English."[80] Active in the affairs of the Conservative Movement, Greenstone served in the 1930's as the Chairman of the Rabbinical Assembly Committee on Jewish Law.[81]

The early Seminary taught *hazzanut* as well as rabbinics, and one individual who successfully combined both fields was Israel Goldfarb, a "rabbi and cantor who contributed greatly to the musical growth of liturgical melody in the synagogue, school, and home in the United States."[82] An instructor of liturgical music at the Seminary for many years, Goldfarb wrote the melody for the hymn "Shalom Aleichem," which is used by Jews around the world on Friday evenings. Other distinguished graduates of the early Seminary were Herman Abramowitz, who served as a rabbi for decades in Montreal and became President of the United Synagogue of America in 1926; Menahem M. Eichler, rabbi in Philadelphia who

---

[79]*AH*, July 4, 1902, p. 184; according to the *Jewish Messenger* (July 4, 1902, p. 6), Nathan Wolf also received the title of *hazzan*.

[80]*Encyclopaedia Judaica* (Jerusalem, 1973), Vol. 7, pp. 911-912.

[81]Rosenblum, *Conservative Judaism*, p. 117.

[82]Nulman, *Jewish Music*, p. 89.

later served as President of the Rabbinical Assembly; Charles H. Kauvar, who was rabbi in Denver for over fifty years and was active in the United Synagogue and the Jewish Welfare Board; and Leon H. Elmaleh, who served as the successor to Sabato Morais at Mikveh Israel in Philadelphia for over half a century.

In summary, the achievements of the early graduates of the Seminary were significant; and most of them pursued long and distinguished careers in the pulpit or in Jewish education. Considering that from the time of the first graduation (1894) to the reorganization of the institution (1902) was only eight years, the results seem even more impressive, shattering the popular notion that the early Seminary was weak and ineffective. Although the early Seminary did not operate a formal Placement Service, congregations seeking rabbis would write in either to the institution itself, or to members of the Advisory Board; and the demand for J.T.S. graduates was always very great.[83]

In June, 1901, at the home of Rabbi M.M. Eichler in Philadelphia, the graduates of the Seminary founded the J.T.S. Alumni Association, with Henry M. Speaker as President, David Wittenberg as Vice President, Eichler as Secretary, Michael Fried as Recording Secretary, and Leon Elmaleh as Treasurer.[84] Founded originally to provide financial support for the Seminary, the Alumni Association grew to become the Rabbinical Assembly, the central organization for the Conservative rabbinate.

In addition to its formal academic program, the Seminary offered several extracurricular activities which added immeasurably to the quality of student life and helped to prepare the young men for the rabbinate. Although the early Seminary had daily religious services, and Sabbath morning services for a time as well, the spiritual highlight of the week was the Saturday afternoon *mincha* service, at which the students had an opportunity to improve both their *hazzanut* and their preaching. Apparently, many of the students preferred to pray in other synagogues on Saturday mornings, so as to be exposed to various preachers and rituals, but on Saturday afternoons at 3:30 P.M., starting in December, 1892, they

---

[83]*AH*, June 24, 1898, p. 225.
[84]Ibid., June 21, 1901, p. 137.

would assemble at the Seminary for what became the main service of the week. Generally, the senior students would take turns preaching during their last few years at the institution, but faculty members, trustees, and members of the Advisory Board, as well as an occasional alumnus, would preach regularly also. The students usually spoke about the afternoon's Torah reading; but occasionally they would speak in more general terms on such varied issues as Zionism, anti-Semitism, and the immortality of the soul. These services were open to the general public; and the *American Hebrew* helped promote them by listing the sermon topics in advance each week and by occasionally printing the full text of the students' discourses.

The students also had frequent opportunities to speak in local synagogues; and many of them assumed pulpits on the High Holidays as well. Occasionally a young man would accept a student pulpit on a regular basis, sometimes remaining there after ordination; and many of the Seminary students also taught in local religious schools, or at institutions like the Educational Alliance or the Y.M.H.A.

Another valuable extracurricular activity at the early Seminary was the Literary Society, which met every two weeks on Saturday evenings. The society was also open to non-Seminary students of both sexes; and, after the fashion of the day, it presented "declamations," essays, poetry readings, musical selections, and debates on a whole range of Jewish and general topics ranging from the Boer War to Zionism and the value of Hasidism. Seminary faculty and trustees often participated actively in the Society; and Professor Joshua Joffe took a special interest, frequently coming to lecture to the students in Hebrew. As judges for their debates, the students often chose distinguished personages from the community, and even the philanthropist Jacob Schiff and Rabbi Gustav Gottheil served in this capacity.[85] In December, 1897, the students formed the Morais Literary Society, in memory of their former mentor; and its meetings were conducted entirely in the Hebrew language, with the students often composing original poems and stories.[86] The English-

---

[85]Ibid., Dec. 8, 1899, p. 183.
[86]Ibid., Dec. 17, 1897, p. 230.

language Literary Society continued to exist as well; and it was renamed the Blumenthal Literary Society in 1901, to honor the memory of the Seminary's first President.[87] Together, these two Literary Societies not only helped the students to sharpen their speaking and writing skills, they also provided the young men with an opportunity to socialize in a Seminary context as well.

Although very little record of it has survived, around the turn of the century a student council, known as the Students' League, was founded at the Seminary.[88] In 1900, its president was Aaron P. Drucker, and he was succeeded in 1901 by Nathan Wolf, and by Charles Kauvar in 1902. Taken altogether, the Seminary's extracurricular activities and services helped to provide the students with a rich Jewish life outside of the classroom; and they also helped to forge bonds of loyalty between the alumni, who often participated in these activities, and their alma mater.

---

[87]*Proceedings*, J.T.S.A., 1902, p. 20.
[88]*AH*, March 2, 1900, p. 10.

CHAPTER V

Seminary and Community

F rom its very inception, the Jewish Theological Seminary of America was deeply committed to the American Jewish community. The primary goal of the Seminary's founders was to combat the doctrines of Reform Judaism, as enunciated in the Pittsburgh Platform, and to provide a traditional alternative to Isaac Mayer Wise's Hebrew Union College. Nevertheless, there were several other community-oriented goals which compelled the attention of the founders. One such goal was that of raising the abysmal level of Jewish education in the United States. On the one hand, the students of the older, established community generally attended the pitifully inadequate Sunday Schools, which the *American Hebrew* labelled a "gigantic sham."[1] On the other hand, the children of the Eastern European immigrants, if they received any Jewish education at all, were usually taught by a *melamed* who was completely out of touch with the modern American culture to which the children were being exposed in the public schools. The result was that most American Jewish children learned very little, if anything, about their heritage; and concerned leaders such as Sabato Morais feared that knowledge of the Bible and of the Hebrew language would soon be lost altogether.[2] To ameliorate this situation by producing rabbis who would also serve as teachers was therefore a high priority of the founders of the Seminary.

Another stated goal of the Seminary founders was to elevate the moral level of many young American Jews, and to raise them from the degenerate pursuits that were pointed out by many an impartial observer. As Joseph Blumenthal noted,

---

[1]*AH*, July 29, 1881, p. 127.
[2]*Proceedings*, J.T.S.A., 1890, p. 28.

> Especially for many of our young men, the club, the race-track, the billiard and drinking-saloon, or even more pernicious attractions have not only great, but almost entire sway over their hours not devoted to the necessary calls of business . . . Their war-cry seems to be, 'Millions for palatial clubhouses, but hardly a dollar for educational or Jewish purposes!'[3]

Thus, by providing a role-model for their contemporaries, it was hoped that both Seminary students and alumni would somehow be able to turn this situation around. In the words of Dr. Morais, "If but a few of the students whom we strive to imbue with righteous sentiments will respond to the constant appeals for loyalty to the Torah . . . and preach it, regardless of the material recognition of clerical services . . . we may not unreasonably found upon strong grounds our expectations for a better future."[4]

Perhaps the most ambitious goal which the Seminary founders enunciated was that of helping to "Americanize" the new immigrants from Eastern Europe. The process of Americanization had two essential components. The first was literally to "civilize" the immigrants, and to make them conform to the ethical, cultural, and aesthetic values of American life. In the words of the *American Hebrew*, "Education is needed, culture and refinement are needed. Frequent contact is necessary for these hapless creatures with the highest, best and purest forces of our civilization. They must be rescued from the sordid ideals which many acquired."[5] Naturally, this aspect of Americanization was rooted in the cultural bias and sometimes overt prejudice which characterized the reaction of the "uptown Jews"towards their "downtown" brethren. To a great degree, this attitude was shaped by self-interest, for the older, established community feared that the immigrants would stir up anti-Jewish feelings and resentment due to their alien ways. Addressing the 1898 Seminary Association Convention, Rev. Henry Morais, the son of the founder of the institution, spoke about this issue directly:

---

[3]*AH*, Feb. 22, 1889, pp. 35-36.

[4]S. Morais, sermon, "On a proposed Sabbath League in N.Y.," *Parshat Yitro*, 1894, Morais Papers.

[5]*AH*, May 3, 1889, p. 214.

Those [Russian] congregations will be either the fame or the shame of American Judaism. They can make the American Judaism of the future equal to the Golden Age of Spanish Judaism in the past. Or they will, by uncouthness, or by infidelity, or by lax ideas of moral right in business or social life, feed the prejudice against us in this country. Our own safety, therefore, demands that we shall not neglect these congregations. Our own interests require that they shall be supplied with ministers who shall be acceptable to them.[6]

The goal of raising the cultural and moral standards of the immigrants and of elevating them from their allegedly degenerate state was only half of the Americanization process as conceived by the founders of the Seminary, although this is all that is generally referred to when the term "Americanization" is employed. The second component of the process was a far more subtle and sophisticated one, for the founders realized that, willy-nilly, Americanization was inevitable for the second generation. What troubled the founders of the Seminary, however, was the fact that they feared that many of the children of the immigrants would grow up without any Jewishness at all. Exposed during the day to the non-sectarian (or Christian) values of the public schools, the youngsters found little to appeal to them in the Eastern European orthodox Judaism of their parents; and the relatively feeble attempts at Jewish education in the ghetto did little to rectify this situation. Thus, the founders of the Seminary saw themselves as spearheading a movement to Americanize the Judaism of the immigrants, by making it more attractive and appealing to the second generation, in order to preserve the Jewish tradition in America. As Henry Pereira Mendes noted at the 1898 Seminary Convention, "American Judaism will be profoundly influenced by Russian Jews, who are establishing hundreds of congregations in the United States. What shall we say to them? 'Be cultured, but combine culture with fidelity to the Torah.'"[7]

In order to implement these goals, it was necessary for the Seminary to reach out to the community, and it did so in several

---

[6]*Proceedings*, J.T.S.A., 1898, p. 32.
[7]*AH*, March 25, 1893, p. 623.

ways. For one thing, the students often accepted High Holiday positions, sometimes in institutions, such as prisons or orphanages, and sometimes in synagogues throughout the eastern United States and Canada. Occasionally, a student would remain in one of these congregations during the year on a part-time basis, and a few of the students, such as Bernard M. Kaplan in Montreal, remained there after ordination. From time to time, the students would be asked to serve as guest preachers in some of the New York synagogues as well.

One interesting proposal, which received the full support of the *American Hebrew*, was that all Seminary students, just prior to ordination, should be compelled to spend a year serving as circuit preachers in certain parts of the country, such as the South or New England, in order to help alleviate the shortage of rabbis in rural areas. Although the newspaper made this suggestion on at least four occasions,[8] the Seminary never dealt with the proposal, probably because of the great expense and planning that such a program would entail.

Another way in which the Seminary students would reach out to the community was by teaching in religious schools and other Jewish institutions in the New York metropolitan area. Students frequently taught at the so-called "mission schools" of the large congregations, which were established in ghetto areas throughout the city, to provide Jewish education to the children of the immigrants. Indeed, one student, Bernard M. Kaplan, actually became the principal of the Shearith Israel Mission School, which was located at the Educational Alliance;[9] and another student, Nathan Wolf, was Superintendent of that congregation's Tremont Jewish Sunday School in the Bronx.[10] In addition to the congregational schools, Seminary students also lectured from time to time at the Y.M.H.A., the Hebrew Sheltering Guardians' Orphan Asylum, the Educational Alliance, and other similar institutions; and they also conducted Friday evening services for a while at the Y.M.H.A.[11]

---

[8]See *AH*, April 5, 1895, p. 626; May 10, 1895, p. 5; May 17, 1895, p. 29; January 3, 1896, p. 254.

[9]Ibid., March 18, 1898, p. 592.

[10]Ibid., Dec. 8, 1899, p. 146.

[11]Ibid., Nov. 2, 1900, p. 715.

Around 1900, some of the students organized an informal group known as the "Jewish Endeavor Society"in order to work directly with young Jewish men and women on the East Side. Later opening branches in Harlem and Yorkville, the Society, whose first president was Herman Abramowitz, was a serious attempt by Seminary students and other concerned individuals to provide meaningful Jewish education to young adults.[12] At the 1900 Seminary Convention, President Blumenthal reported that,

> The students of the Senior Class have also found a field of great usefulness among the young men and women of our faith in the East Side, or downtown portion of our city. A number of societies have been organized for the study of Jewish History and Literature, and week by week these students address large and attentive audiences of that class of our younger co-religionists, who must either receive their impressions and knowledge of the principles of Judaism in the vernacular, and in an intelligent and sensible manner, or go entirely astray from the teachings and practices of our religion.[13]

For a time, the organization conducted a lecture series at the Educational Alliance, sponsored a Religious School for children, and ran a "Young People's Synagogue" at the Forsyth Street Congregation, with sermons delivered by students from the Seminary.[14] Although it won the high praise of Acting President A. S. Solomons at the 1902 Seminary Association Convention,[15] the Jewish Endeavor Society appears to have disbanded within a few years after that time.[16]

Seeking to expand its sphere of influence, as well as to win greater support from the New York Jewish community, the Seminary, from its very inception, tried to provide educational opportunities for the general public, principally through the medium

---

[12]Drachman, *Light*, pp. 225-226; see also Jeffrey S. Gurock, "Resisters and Accommodators: Varieties of Orthodox Rabbis in America, 1886-1983," *American Jewish Archives*, XXXV, no. 2 (Nov., 1983), pp. 114-115.

[13]*Proceedings*, J.T.S.A., 1900, pp. 13-14.

[14]*AH*, March 29, 1901, p. 577; also June 14, 1901, p. 110.

[15]*Proceedings*, J.T.S.A., 1902, p. 12.

[16]Drachman, *Light*, p. 226.

of public lectures. As early as July, 1888, the Seminary presented a well-attended summer lecture series, with Sabato Morais discussing "Post-biblical History," Cyrus Adler giving three lectures on Biblical Archaeology, and Bernard Drachman teaching "the History of Hebrew Grammar." Dr. Adler's talks must have been especially fascinating for the audience, because he discussed the "Creation, Paradise, Deluge, and Genealogical table"of the Bible in comparison to the literature of ancient Babylonia.[17] The following summer, all three instructors returned, with Dr. Drachman now teaching "Jewish Educational Needs and Methods"; and the Rev. Henry Pereira Mendes joined the program, speaking on ancient Jewish history. In 1890, Morais, Adler, and Drachman all taught in the summer program; and they were joined by Alexander Kohut and Marcus Jastrow.

In the winter of 1892, the Seminary launched an ambitious lecture series entitled "The Activities of the Rabbi," which was held on weekday afternoons at the Y.M.H.A. on Lexington Avenue and 58th Street.[18] The lecturers included Sabato Morais, Benjamin Szold, Cyrus Adler, Henry Schneeberger, Bernard Drachman, Marcus Jastrow, Frederick de Sola Mendes, Henry S. Jacobs, and Alexander Kohut—a veritable "who's who" of the Historical School.[19] The speakers discussed almost every conceivable aspect of the rabbinate, and the lectures were very well attended. Nevertheless, despite the success of these lecture programs, the Seminary, possibly for financial reasons, soon ceased to offer them, and confined itself thereafter to occasional lectures on relevant topics.

In October, 1892, shortly after the arrival of Professor Joshua Joffe, the Seminary launched another ambitious project open to the general public, the Amal Torah Society. Meeting at least four evenings a week, this organization was essentially an advanced Talmud study group that proceeded at a very rapid pace. The Society appears to have consisted of at least ten men, several of

---

[17]Instructor's Report from Cyrus Adler to S. Morais, August 20, 1888, Morais Papers.

[18]*AH*, Feb. 26, 1892, p. 71.

[19]Henry Pereira Mendes was also scheduled to speak, but was prevented from doing so when he was shot by a would-be assassin. See *AH*, March 11, 1892, cover page.

whom were members of the Seminary Board of Trustees. By December, 1892, the participants had completed all of the Tractate *Berachot* and were beginning *Shabat*. Although the group had completed more than 200 pages of Gemara by February, 1893,[20] it suddenly disappeared from view, and either stopped meeting or lost its connection with the Seminary around that time.

In addition to presenting lectures and other educational opportunities, the Seminary reached out to the community in several other ways. One such outreach was the involvement of Seminary personnel, on every level, with the fledgling Zionist movement. With the exception of Joseph Blumenthal, whose views on the subject are unknown, Sabato Morais, who yearned for a more religious component in Zionism, and Cyrus Adler, who was lukewarm towards the whole idea, almost every major figure associated with the early Seminary was an active Zionist. Bernard Drachman, Gustave Lieberman, Joshua Joffe, Marcus Jastrow, Benjamin Szold, Henry Pereira Mendes, L. Napoleon Levy (a trustee), Solomon Solis Cohen, Aaron Friedenwald, and Harry Friedenwald (an ardent supporter) were all extremely active in Zionist affairs, with the latter serving for a time as the president of the Federation of American Zionists, and Mendes, Jastrow and A. Friedenwald serving as vice presidents.

Most Seminary students also shared their professors' zeal for Zionism, helping to found, along with students from C.C.N.Y., the Young American Zionists in 1896, and Z.B.T. in 1899. This organization, whose initials stood for the Hebrew words, "Zion b'mishpat tipodeh," "Zion shall be redeemed through justice" (Isaiah 1:27), was "a Zionist fraternity composed of college, university and professional men," and was open to "all Zionists in the United States and Canada, who are over 18 years old and have attended a college, university, or professional school of recognized standing for at least two years."[21] Of its thirteen original officers and board members, eight of them were Seminary students, including the president, David Levine, and the vice president, David Liknaitz, as well as the board member, Julius Greenstone, who went on to become a vice president of the Federation of American Zionists. Within a few

---

[20]*AH*, Feb. 3, 1893, pp. 460-461.
[21]Ibid., March 10, 1899, p. 653.

years, Z.B.T. lost its Zionist character, and ultimately became a regular college fraternity, organized on a social basis. Thus, from its very inception, the Seminary was deeply, albeit unofficially, committed to the Zionist movement; and so it can truly be said that when Solomon Schechter first announced his acceptance of the principles of Zionism in 1905,[22] he was not blazing a new trail, but was rather following in the paths of the Seminary founders.

Another way in which the Seminary reached out to the community was by helping to found and to develop organizations that would promote religious observance and Jewish learning in general. One such organization, whose work was later taken over by the Union of Orthodox Jewish Congregations, was the Jewish Sabbath Observance Association, which was founded at the Seminary in January, 1894. As Sabato Morais noted,

> It is fitting that the Jewish Theological Seminary, solemnly pledged to raise defenders to [sic] Holy Writ, as traditionally received, should bring together into its consecrated building our New York brethren, who are eager to save the fourth commandment of the Decalogue from the scandal of extinction.[23]

The first president of the organization was David M. Piza, Max Cohen was first vice president, Henry Pereira Mendes was second vice president, and Percival Menken was secretary; and other Seminary activists who served as trustees were Bernard Drachman, Joseph Newberger, L. Napoleon Levy, and Marx and Moses Ottinger.[24] The purpose of the Association was two-fold: to promote the observance of the Sabbath, and to aid Sabbath observers in finding employment that would be compatible with their religious beliefs. By December, 1894. the organization had opened an employment bureau on the Lower East Side, had attained an enrollment of over 700 members, and had compiled a list of some 950 employers who closed their businesses on the Sabbath day.[25]

---

[22]Robert E. Fierstien, "Solomon Schechter and the Zionist Movement," *Conservative Judaism*, XXIX, no. 3 (Spring, 1975), pp. 7-8.

[23]Sabato Morais, sermon, "On a proposed Sabbath League."

[24]*AH*, Feb, 2, 1894, p. 408.

[25]Ibid., Dec. 28, 1894, p. 248.

Another organization which the Seminary founders helped to create was the American Jewish Historical Society, which was founded at the Seminary in June, 1892. Among the charter members were Sabato Morais, Cyrus Adler, Marcus Jastrow, and Daniel P. Hays.[26] Within a short time, the Society became an organization of national scope, holding its annual meetings in locations around the country; and although its headquarters was later located at the Seminary for many years, the A.J.H.S. functioned as a totally independent organization. Founded primarily to promote the image of the Jews by demonstrating their role in the forging of American democracy,[27] the Society reflected the same desire for acceptance and Americanization that characterized the actions of many of the founders of the Seminary.

Perhaps the Seminary's most ambitious attempt at reaching out to the community was the involvement of its leaders in the founding of the Union of Orthodox Jewish Congregations of America in 1898. As early as February, 1896, Joseph Blumenthal, Henry Pereira Mendes, and Bernard Drachman had addressed a gathering of delegates from 35 Eastern European orthodox congregations at the Forsyth Street Synagogue in the hopes of creating a congregational union.[28] In May of that year, another meeting was held at the Beth Hamedrash Hagadol on Norfolk Street, but it was not until June, 1898, that the Union was actually organized, at a convention held at Shearith Israel, at 70th Street and Central Park West. The meeting was attended by delegates from approximately fifty congregations; and although some of them had mixed pews and organs, the great majority were strictly orthodox synagogues. Henry Pereira Mendes was chosen as president, Revs. P. Klein, Meldola de Sola, and H. W. Schneeberger were vice presidents, along with the East Side publisher Kasriel Sarasohn, and the secretaries were Max Cohen (English) and I. Buchhalter (Hebrew). Reflecting the typical "uptown" prejudice, no secretary was chosen for the Yiddish language. Among the trustees were the Seminary activists Dr. Solomon

---

[26]Ibid., June 10, 1892, p. 188.

[27]Naomi W. Cohen, *A Dual Heritage; The Public Career of Oscar S. Straus* (Phila., 1969), p. 72.

[28]*AH*, Feb. 28, 1896, p. 490.

Solis Cohen, Dr. Aaron Friedenwald, Rev. Bernard Drachman, S. M. Roeder, L. Napoleon Levy, and Cyrus Adler; and Joseph Blumenthal took an active role as well.[29]

Although the ostensible purpose of the union was to promote the cause of orthodox Judaism in the United States, its founders from the Seminary had a more specific goal in mind. In the words of the *American Hebrew*:

> An orthodox union skillfully guided would tend to awaken a large class of could-be-givers to their responsibilities, and the congregations forming such a union would stand to the Seminary of New York as the constituent congregations of the Hebrew Union stand to the Union College.[30]

In founding the Orthodox Union, therefore, the leaders of the Seminary were not only attempting to assert their leadership over all American orthodoxy—a role which, in typical "uptown" fashion, they felt was rightfully theirs, they were also attempting to build a congregational base for the Seminary.

Nevertheless, as we shall see in the next chapter, popular support for the Seminary on the East Side was rather limited for several reasons; and the "uptown" founders' goals for the Orthodox Union never bore fruit. By the 1900 convention, although Pereira Mendes was still elected president, the Eastern European Jews had definitely taken control of the organization. The guest speaker that year was the "Slutzker Rav"; and Yiddish became the dominant language.[31] Within a few years after the arrival of Dr. Schechter, the Orthodox Union completely repudiated the Seminary in favor of Yeshivat Etz Chaim; and, from the point of view of the J.T.S. leadership, their attempt to organize the orthodox in favor of their cause was in vain.

There is one other way in which the early Seminary reached out to the community, and that is, very simply, the involvement of the Seminary activists in various community endeavors. As we have seen, the members of the Advisory Board were all active pulpit rabbis who certainly generated support for the institution on a

---

[29]Ibid., June 10, 1898, p. 172; June 17, 1898. p. 202.
[30]Ibid., April 1, 1898, p. 640.
[31]Ibid., Jan. 4, 1901, p. 236.

popular level. The officers and trustees of the early Seminary were also deeply involved in the Jewish community; and, for many of them, the level of their commitment to Jewish causes is truly amazing. At the same time, the Seminary trustees were not mere figureheads. They took an active role in the everyday functioning of the institution, getting to know the students, monitoring examinations, and even participating in the Literary Society. A few examples will suffice to show the calibre of the individuals who served as lay leaders of the early Seminary.

Joseph Blumenthal (1834-1901), who served as President of the Seminary Association from 1886 to 1901, was a highly respected public servant. A past president of Shearith Israel and the Y.M.H.A., Blumenthal had served as a member of the Committee of Seventy that brought down the Tweed Ring, served in the New York State Assembly, and was a Commissioner of Taxes for the city.[32] A strictly observant Jew, Blumenthal's zeal for the Seminary was boundless; and his published addresses show him as an articulate spokesman for the spiritual aims of the institution. In his last address to the Seminary Association, Blumenthal humbly declared,

> How well, or badly, I have met the needs of my position and its responsibilities, you, who have so honored me, must judge. That I have sincerely and earnestly striven to carry out the intentions of those who established this Seminary, to make it and keep it faithful to Mosaic Law, and an institution where its students may be filled with a love for and a spirit of fidelity and devotion to the Jewish Law, the character and work of its graduates amply testifies. That many others might have done better I have not the slightest doubt—that I have tried to [do] my whole duty I can solemnly avow. But *you* must do better . . . You can do it—you need only will it. The cause is that of Religion and of God. The blessing of Heaven will reward our efforts.[33]

The Vice President for the entire history of the early Seminary was Dr. Aaron Friedenwald of Baltimore (1836-1902), a distinguished physician who was deeply involved in many Jewish and non-sectarian causes, and who, along with his son, Harry, was

---

[32]Pool, *Old Faith*, p. 318.
[33]*Proceedings*, J.T.S.A., 1900, p. 16.

especially known for his devotion to Zionism. Another physician on the Seminary Board was Dr. Solomon Solis Cohen of Philadelphia (1857-1948), who was a close personal friend and student of Sabato Morais. President of the Philadelphia Y.M.H.A. and active for many years in the Jewish Publication Society, Solis Cohen was a devoted Zionist and a gifted poet and essayist, who wrote frequently on Jewish themes.[34] In addition, Solis Cohen served as Professor of Medicine at the Jefferson Medical College, edited various medical journals, and pioneered in research on typhus and allergies. In his personal life, Solis Cohen was a devout Jew, although not completely observant; and his desire for both tradition and change is reflected in his repeated attempts to persuade Rev. Morais to modernize the liturgy at Mikveh Israel: "Changes will have to come, and as I have so often said to you, unless you make them, they will be made by incompetent hands."[35]

Another Seminary activist who was distinguished for his role in the community was the lawyer, Daniel P. Hays (1854-1923), who was on the Board of Trustees throughout the early Seminary years, and who also served for a time as secretary of the institution. A founder and editorial board member of the *American Hebrew*, Hays was active in the Y.M.H.A., the J.P.S., the Judeans Society, and the Harlem Federation for Jewish Communal Work, and served for years as the president of the traditionalist Reform congregation, Temple Israel of Harlem. In addition, he served for over twenty years as mayor of the village of Pleasantville in Westchester County, where his family had lived for more than a century; and he was also appointed to head the New York City Municipal Civil Service Commission.[36]

Among the other Seminary leaders who were distinguished for their role in the community were Max Cohen (a founder of the *American Hebrew*, active in many Jewish community endeavors), Percival S. Menken (president of the Y.M.H.A.), L. Napoleon Levy (president of Shearith Israel, 1893-1921), and A. S. Solomons (1826-

---

[34]See Davis, *Yahadut Amerika*, pp. 91-97.

[35]Letter from Solomon Solis Cohen to S. Morais, Sept. 18, 1892, Morais Papers.

[36]Cowen, *Memories*, pp. 41-42; *E.J.*, Vol. 7, p. 1504.

1910). A founder and vice president of the American Red Cross, Solomons was a distinguished community activist who succeeded Joseph Blumenthal as Acting President of the Seminary in 1901. President of the New York chapter of the Alliance Israelite Universelle, Solomons was an observant Jew who had helped to found the Mt. Sinai and Montefiore Hospitals and the Hebrew Emigrant Aid Society;[37] and he was also the American representative for the Baron de Hirsch Fund.

As is apparent, the trustees and officers of the early Seminary were influential community leaders, men of standing and prestige in both the Jewish and general worlds. It is often popularly assumed that the early Seminary was run by a group of "non-entities," and that it somehow had to be rescued from oblivion by a coalition of well-known millionaires. In reality, this was not the case, for the trustees of the early Seminary were widely-known and respected personalities. In the next chapter we shall study the problems of the early Seminary and the reasons for its reorganization in 1902. Nevertheless, we would be remiss if we did not raise the question at this point as to why the leaders of the early Seminary, given their prestige in the community, were not more successful in raising support for the institution. The answer is probably two-fold. First, as Solomon Solis Cohen noted many years later, most—but not all—of the Seminary activists were relatively young men, who had yet to make their fortunes and were therefore not in any position to set an example of large giving.[38] Second, many of the early Seminary lay leaders were probably over-extended. Involved in a multitude of community activities, they may have seen the Seminary Association as just another organization, to which they could devote only limited time and resources. Although Joseph Blumenthal's commitment to the Seminary, like that of Sabato Morais, was all-embracing, very few of his colleagues, if any, were willing to follow the splendid example set by the institution's venerable first president.

---

[37]Pool, *Old Faith*, p. 394.
[38]*AH*, April 26, 1912, p. 788.

CHAPTER VI

Problems and Challenges to the Early Seminary

A lthough the early Seminary was successful as an academic
institution, it nevertheless suffered from several problems
that intensified as the years rolled on, and ultimately brought
about its reorganization under new leadership in 1902. Perhaps the
thorniest problem which the Seminary leaders had to confront was
the ever-present lack of funds to maintain the steady growth and
development of the institution. As one studies the financial reports
of the Seminary Association *Proceedings* from 1888 to 1902, it becomes apparent that, although the Seminary was generally not in
danger of bankruptcy, it was severely hampered by the lack of adequate funds which would have permitted the hiring of full-time faculty members and the expansion of services such as library and
classroom facilities.

From its earliest years, the Seminary relied chiefly upon two
sources of revenue—donations from private individuals and contributions from affiliated synagogues. Although the trustees never
made public the initial financial status of the institution, prior to its
opening, Sabato Morais later indicated in a sermon that it raised
barely more than $2,000, most of which came from a gift of Mrs. R.S.
Piza of New York, and from a thousand-dollar donation from
Shearith Israel.[1]

By 1888, the Seminary's financial position had improved somewhat. At that time, the institution had received a total of $8,370.39;
and after disbursements of $2,233.27, the trustees were left with a
balance of $6,137.12.[2] Larger contributions were starting to be re-
ceived, with Jacob Schiff leading the way with a thousand-dollar

---

[1] S. Morais, sermon, "On the Opening of a Higher Class at the J.T. Seminary,"
Dec., 1887, Morais Papers.

[2] *Proceedings*, J.T.S.A., 1888, p. 13.

donation. Although Schiff is generally thought of in connection with the Seminary only after its reorganization, the truth is that, from the earliest days, he was the institution's largest individual donor.

By 1888, twenty congregations had formally joined the Seminary Association, with Alexander Kohut's Ahavath Chesed of New York making an annual donation of $350, followed by Shearith Israel ($250), Mikveh Israel ($200), Chizuk Amuno of Baltimore ($150), Rodeph Sholom of New York ($100), and Shaaray Tefila of New York ($100).[3] In order for a congregation to join the Association, it merely had to pay $15 or $25, depending upon the size of the institution, and for additional $25 donations, the synagogues were entitled to more convention delegates, up to a maximum of ten. Individuals could also join the Association, by paying $5 a year as a subscriber, or $10 as a patron.

Although from the very beginning the Seminary leaders talked about the necessity of raising an endowment fund of $100,000 to support the institution, very little seems to have been done in the early years to make this goal a reality.[4] Nevertheless, in January, 1891, the Seminary embarked upon a major fund-raising campaign, geared especially towards raising sufficient money so as to allow the institution to purchase its own building. The *American Hebrew* took up the cause, and pleaded with its readers for donations:

> The Seminary has come to stay. There is no question as to that. It remains, however, for the Jews of America, and especially of New York, to determine whether it shall be maintained in a manner worthy of the Jewish community.[5]

Seminary campaigns were organized in both New York and Philadelphia; and, by the time of the Seminary Association Convention in April, 1892, the institution had substantially strengthened its financial standing. Receipts from March, 1890 to March, 1892 were $11,254.52, disbursements were $8,430.28, leaving a cash balance of $2,824.24. In addition, the Seminary had established a sinking fund of $5,000 from a bequest of Miss Ellen Phillips;

---

[3]Ibid., p. 25.
[4]See *AH*, March 16, 1888, p. 2.
[5]Ibid., Jan. 30, 1891, cover page.

and it also owned the property in Yonkers, worth $10,000, which had been donated by Sampson Simson to the original Seminary project, many years previously.[6]

Despite the improvement in the overall financial picture, however, the Seminary leaders at the 1892 convention were dismayed by their inability to raise an endowment fund. Dr. Morais lamented that, "the Pizas and the Schiffs ought to have multiplied innumerably," and he asked,

> Why are my fellow-religionists, who should feel it a pride to have in their immediate midst a seat of learning, promising to produce men that will render the Torah honorable throughout America; why are they so tardy in securing for it the mightiest support?[7]

In April, 1893, Jacob Schiff gave $3,000 to help defray the cost of the new Lexington Avenue building; and it seemed as though Morais's pleas were finally bearing fruit. Despite the financial panic of 1893,[8] the Seminary's financial position continued to strengthen; and in its report on the 1894 Seminary Association Convention, the *American Hebrew* noted that,

> The financial status of the Association, though far from enabling the institution from [sic] being placed on an independent and permanent basis, was yet very satisfactory. According to the Treasurer's Report, the income of the Association during the last two years, was something above $21,600; while the disbursements were over $19,000.[9]

Although the 1894 figures reflect a great increase in the Seminary's operating budget, it should be remembered that most of the expenditures involved the new building on Lexington Avenue. From 1892 to 1894, the Seminary spent only $4,303 on faculty salaries, and less than $800 on library facilities. Thus, while the overall financial picture was certainly not a negative one, the institution did not have sufficient funds to permit growth through the

---

[6]*Proceedings*, J.T.S.A., 1892, p. 21.

[7]Ibid., p. 35.

[8]Samuel Eliot Morison, *The Oxford History of the American People* (N.Y., 1965), p. 795.

[9]*AH*, March 30, 1894, p. 650.

hiring of new teaching personnel. Keenly aware of this difficulty, President Blumenthal warned the 1896 convention of an "emergency," and asserted that the Seminary required an additional $3,000 per year in order to sustain its continued growth and development.[10] As the financial situation in the nation deteriorated, donations to the Seminary had shown a pronounced decline; and the receipts from 1894 to 1896 had dropped to less than $15,000, with salaries now totalling one-third of that amount.

By 1898, the Seminary's financial position was sinking precariously. Although Sabato Morais, along with A.S. Solomons and Oscar Straus, had secured a gift of $6,000 from Baroness de Hirsch, the well-known European philanthropist, in June, 1897,[11] Seminary revenues continued to decline, totalling only $15,786.60, including the de Hirsch funds, from 1896 to 1898. At the 1898 convention, President Blumenthal declared that "the burning question" for the Seminary was one of finances, and he launched an impassioned appeal for an annual income of $10,000 for the institution:

> The Seminary must live. It will live. But it is for the Jews of America to say, however, *how* it shall live. Whether it shall limp along half-heartedly doing its work, or walk erect with stout limbs and sturdy frame, performing well its noble task. If Judaism is something more to us than a mere sentiment, if it is a vital fact and a potent factor, then we must realize that the Seminary is an absolute essential to Judaism in America.[12]

After the passing of Sabato Morais in 1897, the Seminary launched a special fund so as to enable it to bring Solomon Schechter to America; and during the years 1898 to 1900, most of the trustees' energies were directed towards building up the Morais Endowment Fund. Regular contributions dropped to a mere $11,000, and President Blumenthal actually made up a deficit of $200 by taking the money out of his own pocket.[13] Taking note of

---

[10]*Proceedings*, J.T.S.A., 1896, p. 19.

[11]*Proceedings*, J.T.S.A., 1898, pp. 13-14.

[12]Ibid., p. 16.

[13]*Proceedings*, J.T.S.A., 1900, p. 20.

the Seminary's declining financial position, the Committee on the Trustees' Report of the 1900 Convention declared,

> Considering the efficiency with which the work of the Seminary has been maintained and the fruits that have already been garnered, we think it nothing less than marvelous that this work should be carried on at an expense of less than six thousand dollars a year. As a matter of fact, we deem it disgraceful that an organization with such purposes and sacred aims should be so hampered and crippled by meagre resources.[14]

The trustees' pleas fell on deaf ears, however, for in the years 1900 to 1902, the Seminary's regular contributions showed no increase. Thus, it is apparent that, by the turn of the century, the Seminary's financial situation had frozen in an unfavorable position; and it was this factor, perhaps more than any other, that led to the institution's reorganization under new leadership in the spring of 1902.

Before concluding the subject of the Seminary's finances, it should be noted that one key pillar of the founders' hopes for the institution was the formation of Seminary Association branches in various cities throughout the country. Unfortunately, however, not enough branches were established; and the ones that were formed, with the exception of the Philadelphia Branch, and, to a much lesser extent, the Baltimore Branch, never raised any sizeable amount of money. Founded largely through the efforts of Sabato Morais and Solomon Solis Cohen, the Philadelphia Branch generally had around one hundred members, and sent approximately $1,500 to the Seminary every two years, with the amount declining steadily towards the turn of the century. Despite the efforts of Benjamin Szold and Henry Schneeberger, the Baltimore Branch usually only managed to raise about half as much money as the Philadelphia organization. Seminary Association branches were also established, generally by alumni, in Syracuse, Buffalo, Cleveland, and Montreal;[15] but the amount of money generated by these organizations was rather small.

---

[14]Ibid., p. 28.
[15]*AH*, June 24, 1898, p. 238.

During the 1890's, an opportunity arose which might have permitted the Seminary to greatly strengthen its financial position; but instead a separate academic institution was established, and the Seminary did not benefit materially. The opportunity occurred in 1893, when a trust fund of almost $150,000, established many years earlier by the late Hyman Gratz, fell to Congregation Mikveh Israel of Philadelphia. The money was to be used for the establishment of a Jewish college in Philadelphia; and various plans were proposed to carry out the terms of Mr. Gratz's will. The *American Hebrew* of New York, always a friend of the Seminary, suggested that the funds be used to help that institution get on its feet:

> We cannot believe that any one who is familiar with the Jewish Theological Seminary in this city will think for a moment that any other disposition of this fund could be made, in accordance with the wishes of the testator, than to place it at the disposal of that institution, whether it be removed to Philadelphia or allowed to remain here.[16]

Henry Pereira Mendes also favored the idea of some sort of merger of the Seminary with the Gratz institution, for in December, 1896, he wrote to the Philadelphia lawyer, Mayer Sulzberger, "I think the Seminary in New York ought to be gradually prepared to be ready to transfer itself to Philadelphia as soon as the Gratz fund and the Seminary resources are together strong enough to maintain it properly."[17]

In Philadelphia, many people wanted to start a full-fledged Jewish University with the Gratz funds, an institution where secular as well as Jewish subjects would be taught.[18] Sabato Morais, however, strongly opposed this proposal, and his views carried the day. Morais envisaged the Gratz institution as teaching only Jewish subjects, and he hoped that it would eventually become a preparatory school for the Seminary: "Promising youths trained here systematically in the written and oral Law, could, when sufficiently advanced, complete their course in the Seminary and graduate from

---

[16]Ibid., Nov. 17, 1893, p. 72.
[17]Whiteman, "Leeser," p. 50.
[18]Davis, *Emergence*, p. 249.

it."[19] Nevertheless, despite the Seminary founders' hopes that the Gratz institution and the Seminary would ultimately be combined in some way, Gratz College was opened as a completely separate institution in 1897, for the purpose of training Hebrew teachers, and its funds were forever lost to the Seminary. The connection between the two schools, however, was very close, for Rabbi Henry Speaker, a member of the Seminary's second graduating class, served as the first principal of Gratz College, a position he held for many years; and Seminary men Isaac Husik and Julius Greenstone were both connected with the Philadelphia school as well.

The early Seminary sought support not only from individuals, but also from synagogues, who were permitted to join the Seminary Association upon payment of either $15 or $25, depending upon the size of the congregation. Although at the Seminary's founding meetings in 1886, several dozen congregations took part in the deliberations, by the time of the first Seminary Association Convention in 1888, the number had dropped to 25. For the next decade, until 1900, the numbers fluctuated between 20 and 25; but at the 1902 Convention, perhaps because of the uncertainty surrounding the future of the institution, only ten congregations were represented.[20] In general, New York would have six or seven congregations represented, Philadelphia would have five or six, Baltimore—three or four, and the remaining congregations were usually in Paterson, Pittsburgh, Syracuse, Louisville, Washington, D.C., Galveston, and Newport.

As to the ideology of the Seminary-affiliated synagogues, they generally represented as broad a spectrum of the American Jewish community as did the rabbis of the institution's Advisory Board. Among the more traditional congregations were H.P. Mendes's Shearith Israel and Drachman's Zichron Ephraim, both of New York, Morais's Mikveh Israel of Philadelphia, and Schneeberger's Chizuk Amuno of Baltimore. Leaning more towards Reform were Kohut's, and later Davidson's, Ahavath Chesed of New York, Jastrow's Rodef Shalom of Philadelphia, and Szold's Oheb Sholom of Baltimore. The openly Reform New York congregation, Temple

---

[19]S. Morais, untitled, undated essay on Gratz College, Morais Papers.

[20]*Proceedings*, J.T.S.A., 1902, p. 10.

Israel of Harlem, also joined the Seminary Association, principally because of the Seminary involvement of its president, Daniel P. Hays. Congregations which supported the Seminary Association, after the earliest years, were generally not populated by Eastern European immigrants. The Seminary congregations tended to serve prosperous, well-established members of the Jewish community, many of whom were either Sephardic or German in origin.

Much has been made of the fact that, as time went on, most of the synagogues affiliated with the Seminary were pulled either to the right or the left, leaving the institution without a viable congregational base. As Herbert Parzen has noted,

> The conclusion is inevitable that the association organized to establish the Seminary and to resist Reform was ephemeral. It could not endure because it was a heterogeneous body held together by a negative purpose, opposition to Reform. As a matter of fact the rabbis of the left wing congregations who, for various reasons, were unable or unwilling to accept the Pittsburgh Platform were principally responsible for associating their congregations with the Seminary. As long as they lived their people followed them; as soon as they died their synagogues forsook the Seminary and embraced Reform.[21]

To some degree, this is an accurate assessment, for both Aaron Wise and Marcus Jastrow were succeeded by Reform rabbis, Frederick de Sola Mendes himself veered towards Reform, while Shearith Israel and Zichron Ephraim in New York ultimately turned towards orthodoxy, as their rabbis, Pereira Mendes and Drachman, broke with the Seminary during the Schechter period. Nevertheless, it should be pointed out that the major problem was not that the Seminary was losing support by 1900, but rather that, from the very beginning, its leaders had failed to organize their supporters into a cohesive unit, comparable to the Union of American Hebrew Congregations. Isaac Mayer Wise had had the wisdom to found the Union before the College; and, by 1900, it had approximately 100 congregations.[22] The Seminary leaders, on the other hand, made no attempt to form a union of traditionalist synagogues, either before

---

[21]Herbert Parzen, *Architects of Conservative Judaism* (N.Y., 1964), p. 23.
[22]Meyer, "Centennial History," p. 32.

or after the founding of the Seminary. Their attempt to form an Orthodox Union in 1898 was a feeble step in the right direction; but by then, as we shall see, the Seminary had already lost support among the Eastern European orthodox Jews. In fairness to the founders of the Seminary, it may be said that they realized how divergent the synagogues that supported it truly were—and, indeed, some of them actually belonged to the U.A.H.C.—but whatever their reasons, their failure to organize a synagogue union proved a real detriment to the subsequent growth of the early Seminary.

The one group that could have provided a substantial source of congregational and, to a lesser extent, financial support for the early Seminary was the Eastern European immigrant Jewish community; but, unfortunately, its interest in the institution was, at best, lukewarm. From the very beginning, ultra-orthodox immigrant leaders, such as J.D. Eisenstein, were upset by the fact that moderate Reformers, such as Alexander Kohut, were allowed to participate in the founding of the Seminary;[23] and, as the years rolled on, these attacks increased. The Seminary did, indeed, have its literary supporters on the Lower East Side, namely the two Yiddish papers published by Kasriel H. Sarasohn, *Die Judische Gazetten* and the *Judisches Tageblatt*;[24] but even these influential periodicals were unable to raise the interest level of the immigrants towards the new institution.

In addition to the involvement of the moderate Reform element, there were several other reasons why the immigrants generally did not support the Seminary. The first and foremost reason why the Seminary could not muster more support on the Lower East Side was the fact that, in the eyes of the immigrants, it was perceived as an "uptown" institution. Although men such as Morais, Pereira Mendes, and Drachman were respected by the immigrants for their piety, if not for their learning, they and their congregations were seen as part of another world, separated by economic, social, cultural, and even linguistic barriers from the Yiddish-speaking

---

[23]Eisenstein, *Ozar Zikhronothai*, p. 209.

[24]See, e.g., *Judisches Tageblatt*, March 6, 1888, page 1. The paper presents a lengthy account of a pro-Seminary meeting, headed by Dr. H.P. Mendes, and then goes on to call for increased congregational support for the new institution.

masses. With English as its language of instruction, the Seminary, almost by definition, was alien to the immigrants, whose only exposure to higher Jewish education had been the Eastern European *yeshiva*, where Yiddish was the primary language. As an example of how far removed the Seminary leaders were from the world of the immigrants, their appeals for funds in the Yiddish newspapers were generally published in English, thereby limiting their impact to only the more Americanized elements of the community.[25]

On a more serious level, the Seminary aroused the suspicions of the orthodox because it was so different from an Eastern European-style *yeshiva*, where Talmud and Codes formed the core of the curriculum, occupying almost all of the student's time. At the Seminary, Bible was a central part of the curriculum; and the teaching of subjects such as Midrash, Jewish History, Philosophy, Hebrew Grammar, and Homiletics, while not inherently untraditional, certainly gave the Seminary students a program which was vastly different from that of their Eastern European counterparts. Indeed, one of the main criticisms of the orthodox was the allegation that Seminary students did not study enough Talmud; and the orthodox newspaper *Ha-Ivri* once even went so far as to claim (incorrectly) that the Senior students at the Seminary had studied only seventeen pages of the Talmud in an entire year.[26] It was in reply to such criticisms that, in 1895, as the *American Hebrew* reported, "Dr. Joffe, instructor of Talmud, has drawn up a list of 500 men versed in Hebrew lore, of whom he will invite in rotation ten or fifteen for each Sunday morning to witness the manner in which the students do justice to the ancient lights of Judaism and the mastery they have gained over the contents of the Talmud."[27] In September, 1899, the Seminary held a public examination in Talmud, announcing that, "Visitors will be invited to suggest any portion of the Talmud for sightreading"by the Seniors.[28] Nevertheless, despite these attempts at demonstrating the Talmudical prowess of its stu-

---

[25]See, e.g., *Judisches Tageblatt*, Dec. 24, 1897, p. 5.

[26]*Ha-Ivri*, Sept. 17, 1897, p. 1a; Oct. 15, 1897, p. 1e, quoted in Klaperman, *Story*, p. 40.

[27]*AH*, Sept. 27, 1895, p. 522.

[28]Ibid., Sept 15, 1899, p. 580.

dents, the perception persisted among many East Siders that the Seminary graduates were not adequately prepared.

In addition, the members of the Seminary faculty all possessed thorough secular educations, which rendered them untraditional in the minds of many orthodox Jews. At the 1902 commencement, the writer for the *Judische Welt* was scandalized by the fact that several Seminary professors sat with uncovered heads, and Professor Joshua Joffe even mentioned God's name without wearing a hat or a yarmulke.[29]

The attitude of the immigrants towards the Seminary is perhaps best expressed in a remarkable letter to the *American Hebrew* from Elias L. Solomon, a Seminary student, who was trying to organize an alumni association for the Machazekei Talmud Torah School on East Broadway. Lamenting that the East Siders do not give generously towards either institution, Solomon observed,

> In the case of the Seminary our down-town co-religionists may be justified in refusing to give aid to an institution concerning the work of which they know but little. Inasmuch as the Seminary is situated up-town, and consequently in that part of the city for which down-town orthodox Jews have a religious abhorrence because it appears to breed reform, atheism, and what not, there may be some ground for the suspicion that the Seminary is a Reform School, a Missionary School, or anything else abominable to our sensitive brethren of the East Side. In fact, I am even willing to excuse the recent arrivals from across the Atlantic who refer to the Seminary as the Jewish Theological Cemetery, and I am ready to admit that this confusion of terms is not due to ignorance, but that it is a wilful perversion intentionally made by those who suspect the Seminary, instead of being an institution seeking to spread the living truths of Judaism, even of that form of it to which they themselves adhere, consists of a faculty and students, dead to the beauty and sublimity of our time-hallowed customs.[30]

The following week, Mr. L. Robison, the principal of the Machazekei Talmud Torah, wrote in to thank Mr. Solomon for his

---

[29]*Judische Welt*, July 3, 1902, p. 4; Klaperman, *Story*, p. 58.
[30]*AH*, Nov. 17, 1899, p. 42.

efforts on behalf of his alma mater; and he concluded his letter with a totally opposite observation:

> Permit me to conclude this communication with a few words in refer-
> ence to deep-seated antipathy, which Mr. Solomon avers exists among
> the East Siders towards the Jewish Theological Seminary. So far as my
> personal knowledge is concerned—and my knowledge of the East Side
> Jewish sentiment on the subject, I may justly claim, is of a rather exten-
> sive nature—the attitude towards the Seminary, far from being inimi-
> cal, is very favorable and sympathetic... As a matter of fact it is the
> only seat of Jewish learning in this country whose graduates are
> looked upon as worthy of occupying the high position of orthodox
> rabbi.[31]

While it is senseless to take sides in this controversy almost ninety years later, it is important to note that Elias Solomon was complaining chiefly about the lack of *material* support for the Seminary on the part of the immigrants; and about this there is no question.

Although the Seminary leaders made repeated attempts to raise funds on the East Side, their appeals largely fell upon deaf ears. The 1890 and 1892 Seminary Association *Proceedings* list Chief Rabbi Jacob Joseph as one of the financial subscribers to the institution;[32] but with the Chief Rabbi himself enmeshed in controversy over kashruth supervision and other matters, he could do little to inspire others to give. Indeed, Seminary leaders such as Sabato Morais and H.P. Mendes were themselves originally not in favor of the Chief Rabbi, who was brought to America by a coalition of New York orthodox synagogues in 1888, because they felt that he would divert funds that might be better used by their institution.[33]

In addition, the Seminary had to compete with several other schools for the limited charity contributions of the East Side. The very same year that the Seminary was founded, 1886, an ultra-orthodox day school, Yeshivat Etz Chaim, was established to serve the immigrants; and, along with the Machazekei Talmud Torah, it must surely have served to diminish the immigrants' contributions

---

[31]Ibid., Nov. 24, 1899, p. 86.
[32]*Proceedings*, J.T.S.A., 1890, p. 58; 1892, p. 50.
[33]Karp, "Chief Rabbi," pp. 149-150.

to the Seminary. In 1897, the Rabbi Isaac Elchanan Theological Seminary, which later grew to become Yeshiva University after incorporating Yeshivat Etz Chaim, was established on East Broadway; and it, too, served to divert funds from the Seminary. A conscious attempt to duplicate the Eastern European *yeshiva* on American soil, R.I.E.T.S. grew rapidly. By 1902, it had approximately 70 students, and "an anticipated budget of about $10,000 per year."[34] When one takes into account how little concerned the immigrants of the Lower East Side generally were with respect to Jewish education as well as the struggle that many of them endured just to survive, it becomes apparent that the Seminary's pleas for financial support from the immigrants could never have succeeded, particularly when it had to compete with Yeshivat Etz Chaim and R.I.E.T.S. In the last chapter we spoke about how the Seminary leaders founded the Union of Orthodox Jewish Congregations in 1898, in an attempt to win more support from the immigrants. Nevertheless, when we realize the tremendous barriers that separated the Seminary and its supporters from the world of the immigrant masses, it appears inevitable that the Seminary and the orthodox would ultimately go their different ways.

So far, we have discussed the external problems that confronted the early Seminary, the lack of funds and the lack of congregational support, but the greatest challenge that confronted the institution was internal—a crisis of leadership. When Alexander Kohut died in 1894, the early Seminary lost its most prestigious scholar and a rabbi who had the potential to marshall the forces of moderate Reform on behalf of the school. In November, 1897, Sabato Morais also died; and, as the acknowledged leader of traditional Judaism in America, his passing meant not only the loss of an indefatigable worker on behalf of the Seminary, but also of a man who conferred tremendous prestige upon the institution. Finally, in 1901, the tireless President Joseph Blumenthal also passed away, depriving the Seminary of its most gifted and devoted lay leader.

To make matters worse, Morais and Blumenthal were succeeded, respectively, by Henry Pereira Mendes and A.S. Solomons, both of whom consented to serve only on a temporary or "acting"

---

[34]Klaperman, *Story,* p. 65.

basis. Mendes was a busy congregational rabbi, involved in many community endeavors, and he did not have adequate time to devote to the Seminary. A highly successful businessman, Solomons was also deeply involved in community affairs; and he had even less time than Mendes for the Seminary because he lived in Washington, D.C.

The crisis of leadership, however, actually began long before the passing of Kohut, Morais, and Blumenthal. From the very beginning, it was apparent to all the Seminary leaders that the institution suffered from the fact that it did not employ what was termed a "resident dean," a prestigious scholar and teacher who would serve the school on a full-time basis. Thus, the trustees' repeated efforts to induce Morais to move to New York were not only motivated by a solicitude for his health, but also by a strong desire to have full-time leadership at the Seminary.

With the passing of Morais, the need for a full-time President of the Faculty became imperative. Henry Pereira Mendes and David Davidson assumed "the task of supervising the pedagogic work at the institution,"[35] but they were both busy congregational rabbis and did not have the time which the Seminary required. Thus, the trustees immediately resolved to establish a fund in memory of the Seminary's beloved founder, for the express purpose of securing a full-time head of the institution. As Joseph Blumenthal proclaimed at the 1898 Seminary Association Convention,

> It is proposed to collect a Morais Endowment Fund sufficiently large to endow a professorship in the Seminary. It is hoped that thus a permanent basis may be given to the institution, so that an incumbent may be secured whose scholarship and character will command for him and the Seminary the respect of all who would have the institution with the highest of its class, and the support of those who would insure for the Jews in America a body of earnest, well-equipped spiritual leaders and religious teachers.[36]

---

[35]*Proceedings*, J.T.S.A., 1898, p. 13.
[36]Ibid., p. 13.

With the active support of the *American Hebrew*, the Morais Fund got off to a good start. Several fund-raising meetings were held, and Jacob Schiff gave $5,000.[37]

As the search for a successor to Morais went on, a very interesting proposal was made in 1900, when the editors of the *American Hebrew* published a symposium on the question of whether there should be a merger between the Hebrew Union College and the Seminary.[38] With the passing of Isaac Mayer Wise in 1900, both institutions were left without the leadership of their distinguished founders; and so the anonymous proposal to merge the two institutions did have some practical value. Among those answering in the affirmative were Jacob Schiff, Simon Wolf, and Louis Marshall, who, with a monumental insensitivity to theology, wrote, "The differences between these kindred institutions relate to matters of form only. Their attitude towards fundamental doctrines and principles is in no sense antagonistic."[39] Of the individuals actively involved with the two schools, only Professor Gotthard Deutsch of H.U.C. approved the proposal. Opposing the merger idea were such varied leaders as Reform Rabbis Max Heller and Rudolf Grossman, as well as Seminary activists Bernard Drachman, Solomon Solis Cohen, Henry Morais, and Cyrus Adler, who branded the entire proposal "a waste of time." At no time did the leaders of the two schools seriously consider the proposal; and, indeed, given the vast theological and halachic differences between the two institutions, it is somewhat surprising that the *American Hebrew* even considered the question, unless the editors hoped to demonstrate its impossibility in that manner. If there is anything that the symposium did demonstrate, it was that the Seminary would have to survive on its own efforts, and it must surely have strengthened the resolve of the trustees to find the ideal leader for the institution.

In the 1900 Seminary Association *Proceedings*, the members of the Advisory Board listed four qualities which the new head of the Seminary must possess: 1. he must be loyal to "historical Judaism"; 2. he must possess "executive ability" so as to increase congrega-

---

[37]*AH*, Jan. 21, 1898. p. 359.
[38]Ibid., May 25, 1900, pp. 36-40; June 1, 1900, pp. 69-72.
[39]Ibid., May 25, 1900, p. 40.

tional support for J.T.S.; 3. he must be a renowned scholar; 4. "he shall not be attached to any congregation in any official capacity, as otherwise the interests of the Seminary would suffer."[40] Despite the fact that the trustees appeared to be searching for a proper candidate, from the very beginning there was really only one man whom they desired to head the Seminary—Solomon Schechter. A distinguished member of the faculty of Cambridge University in England, Schechter had attained a world-wide reputation as a scholar for his efforts in rescuing the contents of the Cairo Genizah, as well as for his brilliant books, written on both a scholarly and popular level.

According to Rebekah Kohut, as early as 1888, Alexander Kohut had travelled to London to "invite Professor Schechter to come to America as the head of the faculty of the Jewish Theological Seminary as arranged by Sabato Morais, Jacob H. Schiff and himself."[41] Nevertheless, after consulting with his friend, Claude Montefiore, Schechter decided, probably for financial reasons, "that the time was not yet ripe . . . to leave England." Although Mrs. Kohut's memory may have been faulty when she wrote that the Seminary leaders desired Schechter to head the institution at such an early date, they surely wanted him on the faculty, for in 1890, at the urging of Morais and Blumenthal, Solomon Solis Cohen once again tried unsuccessfully to persuade Schechter to come to America.[42]

In February, 1895, Schechter became widely known to the American Jewish public when he travelled to Philadelphia to deliver a series of lectures on Rabbinic Theology sponsored by the Gratz Fund. The talks, which were repeated in Baltimore at Johns Hopkins University, were very well received; and the visit to America gave Schechter the opportunity to strengthen his acquaintance with Mayer Sulzberger and Cyrus Adler, both of whom were later influential in persuading him to come to the Seminary.[43]

After the passing of Sabato Morais in November, 1897, it became even more imperative to engage a full-time head of the Seminary,

---

[40]*Proceedings*, J.T.S.A., 1900, p. 19.

[41]R. Kohut, *My Portion*, p. 139.

[42]Solis Cohen, "J.T.S. Past and Future," pp. 34-35.

[43]Abraham J. Karp, "Solomon Schecter Comes to America," *AJHQ*, LIII, no. 1 (Sept., 1963), p. 48.

and Solomon Schechter was the logical and unanimous choice of the trustees. Not only was he an outstanding scholar, he wrote and spoke English fluently, and his moderate traditionalist outlook fit in well with the religious posture of the leaders of the Seminary. As the *American Hebrew* noted in 1900, "Dr. Schechter is probably the one man who can best fill the post of President of a Jewish Seminary in America . . . He is scientific and progressive; he lives the life of an orthodox Jew."[44]

The process by which Solomon Schechter and the Seminary trustees negotiated the conditions for his coming to America has been thoroughly described by Professor Abraham J. Karp.[45] Suffice it here to say that largely through the efforts of Mayer Sulzberger, along with Cyrus Adler, Solomon Solis Cohen, Charles Hoffman, Leonard Lewisohn, and others, Schechter was ultimately persuaded to leave Cambridge in 1902 and to accept the position of President of the Faculty of the reorganized Seminary.[46] The negotiations were long and difficult, chiefly because Schechter wanted to be assured of his financial security; and from time to time, false hopes were raised, as in December, 1899, when the *American Hebrew* proudly announced that Schechter had accepted the call, only to retract the article a month later, when it became clear that the negotiations were not concluded.[47] Part of the problem was the fact that the Morais Endowment Fund, after a good beginning, did not raise sufficient money to guarantee Schechter's contract;[48] and it was this financial weakness, more than anything else, which provided the opening for a new group of individuals to reorganize the Seminary and take over its leadership.

---

[44]*AH*, Jan. 12, 1900, p. 320.

[45]See Karp, "Solomon Schechter Comes to America."

[46]Charles I. Hoffman, "Memories of Solomon Schechter," in *J.T.S. Semi-Centennial Volume*, pp. 49-50.

[47]*AH*, Dec. 15, 1899, p. 205; Jan. 12, 1900, p. 321.

[48]Ibid., Dec. 13, 1901, p. 133.

CHAPTER VII

Epilogue

On Sunday, March 30, 1902, at the Biennial Convention of the Jewish Theological Seminary Association, the delegates formally voted to merge with the newly-formed corporation, called "The Jewish Theological Seminary of America," thereby sanctioning the reorganization of their beloved Seminary.[1] Although the details of the reorganization itself and the motivations of its protagonists lie beyond the scope of this study, suffice it to say that the reorganization of the Seminary was a carefully planned and executed procedure, which was skillfully initiated by Adolphus S. Solomons and Cyrus Adler. In his autobiography and in the *J.T.S. Semi-Centennial Volume*, Adler relates how he was present at a party at the home of Isidor Straus on upper Broadway in 1901:

> There was a small group standing together and they were speaking of Jewish affairs in New York, and particularly of Jewish education. I said, possibly in an off-hand and breezy sort of way, as young men are likely to do, that the Jewish community in New York, which was destined to be the largest community in the world, was allowing its only institution of higher Jewish learning to perish, and I told them something about the precarious situation of this Seminary. Mr. Schiff, who was a man of quick decisions, said to the men standing around, 'Dr. Adler is right,' and a few weeks later I received a letter from him, asking me when I was coming to New York next time, so that he might invite a few men to meet with us.[2]

Nevertheless, in his biography of Jacob Schiff, Adler gives a very different description of the origin of the reorganization: "It was

---

[1]*AH*, April 4, 1902, pp. 596-600.
[2]Cyrus Adler, "Semi-Centennial Address," in *J.T.S. Semi-Centennial Volume*, p. 9.

primarily Solomons who brought to Schiff's attention the need for making a stronger institution of the Seminary."[3] Although both accounts were written many years after the events, it seems likely that Adolphus S. Solomons was the prime mover of the reorganization because he was Acting President at the time, and, as a wealthy, well-connected businessman, his words would have had a great impact on the millionaires who ultimately rescued the Seminary. In addition, in a 1901 letter to Solomon Schechter, Adler mentioned that Jacob Schiff and others had considered reorganizing the Seminary as early as 1899, long before the party at Isidor Straus's home.[4]

One of the immediate causes for the reorganization of the Seminary was the fact that the Morais Endowment Fund did not raise sufficient money to allow for the hiring of Solomon Schechter; and it was at this juncture that Solomons, Adler, and the Seminary trustees turned to Jacob Schiff and his friends, looking for help. In return for their money, these Reform Jews of German origin demanded almost complete and permanent control of the Seminary. Not only was Solomon Schechter to serve as President of the Faculty, Cyrus Adler was to become the chief "Executive Officer" of the institution, and Louis Marshall was to become Chairman of the Board of Directors.[5] Two classes of directors were established, and only the philanthropists would be eligible for the permanent posts of "Class A." For their part, Schiff and his friends agreed to endow the Seminary lavishly. Schiff alone gave $100,000, and promised to erect a new Seminary building on Morningside Heights, near Columbia University. Leonard Lewisohn gave $50,000, as did the Guggenheim brothers, Isaac, Morris, Simon, and Daniel.[6] These sums, of course, far exceeded anything that the old Seminary trustees had been able to raise; and it was this prospect of financial salvation that caused them to relinquish their authority and to accept the reorganization proposal.

---

[3]Cyrus Adler, *Jacob H. Schiff: His Life And Letters* (N.Y., 1928), Vol. II, p. 53.

[4]Letter, Cyrus Adler to Solomon Schechter, August 26, 1901, in Cyrus Adler, *Selected Letters*, ed. Ira Robinson (Phila./N.Y., 1985), Vol. I, pp. 90-91.

[5]*AH*, April 4, 1902, p. 598.

[6]Ibid., Dec. 13, 1901, p. 138.

The records of the March 30, 1902 meeting indicate that the reorganization plan was accepted only with great bitterness and resentment on the part of some of the old trustees:

> Mr. Max Cohen complained of the treatment of the old Seminary Association; it should have been treated with the dignity and respect which its history deserved, it should have been consulted when the preliminary steps were being taken; it should not have been confronted with a cut and dried agreement.[7]

Nevertheless, after all the debate, the merger proposal passed unanimously, for the trustees of the old Seminary knew very well that the reorganization was the only viable way to save the institution. The only demand that the trustees made was that the new leaders of the Seminary should agree to conduct the institution on the basis of Article II of the Seminary Association Constitution, which guaranteed the Seminary's loyalty to "historical Judaism." With the conclusion of the 1901-1902 academic year and the graduation on July 1, the old Seminary gave way to the new.

With the completion of the reorganization process, the Seminary became a very different institution. Sabato Morais had been a learned congregational rabbi, Solomon Schechter was a professional scholar and gave a different tone to the institution. Instead of a largely unpaid, part-time faculty, Schechter assembled a full-time teaching staff composed of outstanding young scholars such as Louis Ginzberg, Alexander Marx, Israel Friedlaender, Mordecai Kaplan, and Israel Davidson. Under Schechter, the Seminary became a graduate school, and the students were academically more mature. In terms of its lay leadership, a new array of individuals became involved in the institution, men such as Louis Marshall and Mayer Sulzberger, who had been only peripherally involved, if at all, with the early Seminary.

Writing at the time of the reorganization of the Seminary, Daniel P. Hays had asserted that, "It will no longer be known as an orthodox seat of learning, but Judaism will be its corner stone, and Hebrew Language, literature and history, its foundation."[8]

---

[7]Ibid., April 4, 1902, p. 600.
[8]Ibid., April 11, 1902, p. 686.

Although the new Seminary leaders took exception to Hays's remarks, in the long run he proved correct; for under Solomon
Schechter the Seminary gradually became a "Conservative" institution, losing its ties to the orthodox. Given the experiences of the
early Seminary with the Eastern European orthodox, this result was
probably inevitable; and, in addition, the early Seminary was a
multi-faceted institution, better described as "traditional" than as
"orthodox."

It might be asked why it was that the early Seminary graduates
did not seek or accept positions in immigrant congregations, which
would have exerted a right-wing pull on the institution at the time
of Schechter's arrival. The answer, however, is very simple: first, the
ghetto congregations generally could not have afforded to pay
sufficient salaries to attract Seminary graduates. Second, for its
students, the Seminary was a way out of the ghetto, and its college-
educated graduates felt no compulsion or desire to return. Thus, as
the Seminary became more "Conservative" during the Schechter
years, it encountered little opposition from the early graduates,
whose congregations frequently mirrored the same transformations.

As an academic institution, the early Seminary has largely been
ignored. Although its founding and reorganization have attracted
scholarly attention, the institution itself has not, generally being described in only one or two sentences. Yet, as we have seen, the early
Seminary was a respectable institution of higher learning, that
sought to imbue its students with a broad understanding of the
Jewish tradition. In its emphasis on Bible, Midrash, Homiletics,
Jewish History, Philosophy, and spoken Hebrew, as well as Talmud
and Codes, the early Seminary anticipated much of the curriculum
of the modern-day Seminary; and professors such as Alexander
Kohut and Joshua Joffe introduced the students to critical methodology in much the same way that modern professors do. It should
be remembered that Solomon Schechter did not come to a new institution, which he might not have been willing to do, given the risks
involved. In addition, it was leaders of the old Seminary, such as
Morais, Kohut, and Solis Cohen, who first interested Schechter in
the institution, long before the philanthropists got involved.

Not only in its academic aspects was the early Seminary a vital
institution, but also in its extracurricular programs as well. Its free

public lecture series made it a recognized factor in the community, as did the personal service efforts of its students in preaching and teaching throughout the metropolitan area. In Zionism, in Jewish education, even in social work, the early Seminary students did make a difference in the life of the community.

Although it would not be correct to say that the Conservative Movement began in the early Seminary, the institution surely helped to pave the way for the development of Conservative Judaism by providing a cadre of modern, university-trained, American rabbis, whose outlook was very different from that of the Eastern European orthodox, especially with regard to such areas as aesthetics, Jewish education, and attitude towards secular learning. Although there were many changes under Solomon Schechter, there was an essential continuity at the Seminary as well, a devotion to Jewish learning and to the Jewish community that has remained constant down to this day, as well as a commitment to the broad educational program developed at Breslau. As the Jewish Theological Seminary enters its second century, it can look back with pride on its modest beginning, and see the value in the noble endeavor that was the early Seminary.

BIBLIOGRAPHY

Archival Material

Annenberg Research Institute: The Papers of Sabato Morais, Letters of Mayer Sulzberger.

The Jewish Theological Seminary of America: Letters of Jacob Schiff and Mayer Sulzberger.

Interview

Interview with Mr. Joseph Elmaleh, son of Rev. Leon H. Elmaleh, Dec. 26, 1983.

Periodicals

American Hebrew, 1879-1903.

American Israelite, 1882-1900.

Jewish Messenger, 1883-1892.

Jewish Record, 1883-1886.

Judisches Tageblatt, 1888-1898.

Primary Sources

Adler, Cyrus. *I Have Considered the Days*, Philadelphia, 1941.

_____. *Selected Letters*, ed. Ira Robinson, Phila./N.Y., 1985, Vol. 1.

Ben-Horin, Meir. "Solomon Schechter to Judge Mayer Sulzberger," *JSS*, Vol. 27, no. 2 (April, 1965), pp. 75-102.

"Biographical Sketches of Jews Prominent in the Professions, Etc. in the United States," *AJYB*, 5665, 1904, pp. 52-225.

"Biographical Sketches of Rabbis and Cantors Officiating in the United States," *AJYB*, 5664, 1903, pp. 40-108.

Cowen, Philip. *Memories of An American Jew*, N.Y., 1932.

Deutsch, Gotthard. *Modern Orthodoxy; In the Light of Orthodox Authorities*, Chicago, 1898.

Drachman, Bernard. *The Unfailing Light; Memoirs of an American Rabbi*, N.Y., 1948.

Eisenstein, Judah David. *Ozar Zikhronothai: Autobiography and Memoirs*, N.Y., 1929.

Hapgood, Hutchins. *The Spirit of the Ghetto: Studies of the Jewish Quarter of New York*, N.Y., 1965 (1902).

Jewish Theological Seminary Association. *Constitution and By-Laws*, N.Y., 1886.

_____. *Proceedings*, N.Y., 1888-1904.

Kohut, Alexander. *Prayers for the Divine Services of Congregation Ahawath Chesed*, trans. Alexander Kohut, arranged by Dr. A. Huebsch, N.Y., 1889.

Kohut, Rebekah. *As I Know Them, Some Jews and a Few Gentiles*, Garden City, N.Y., 1929.

_____. *My Portion*, N.Y., 1925.

Philipson, David. *Centenary Papers And Others*, Cincinnati, 1919.

_____. "The History of the Hebrew Union College," in *Hebrew Union College Jubilee Volume (1875-1925)*, Cincinnati, 1925, pp. 1-70.

_____. *My Life As An American Jew: An Autobiography*, Cincinnati, 1941.

Sarna, Jonathan D., ed. and trans. *People Walk on Their Heads, Moses Weinberger's 'Jews and Judaism in New York'*, N.Y., 1982.

Solis Cohen, Solomon. "A Seminary Ideal," N.Y., 1919.

_____. "The Jewish Theological Seminary, Past and Future," N.Y., 1919.

Szold, Benjamin; Jastrow, Marcus; and Hochheimer, Henry. *Avodat Yisrael, Israelitish Prayer Book For All The Public Services of The Year*, Phila., 1885.

Voss, Carl Herman, ed. *Stephen S. Wise: Servant of The People*, Phila., 1970.

Weinberger, Moshe. *HaYehudim vi-ha-Yahadut b'New York*, N.Y., 1887.

Wise, Isaac Mayer. *Reminiscences*, trans. David Philipson, N.Y., 1945.

Secondary Sources

Adler, Cyrus. *Jacob H. Schiff: His Life and Letters*, Garden City, N.Y., 1948 (2 vols.).

_____, ed. *The Jewish Theological Seminary of America Semi-Centennial Volume*, N.Y., 1939.

Appel, John J. "The Treyfa Banquet," *Commentary*, February, 1966, pp. 73-78.

Bentwich, Norman. *Solomon Schechter: A Biography*, Phila., 1938.

Brann, M. *Geschichte des Judisch-Theologischen Seminars (Fraenckel'sche Stiftung) In Breslau*, Breslau, 1904.

Chyet, Stanley F. "Isaac Mayer Wise: Portraits by David Philipson," in *A Bicentennial Festschrift for Jacob Rader Marcus*, ed. Bertram W. Korn. N.Y., 1976, pp. 77-92.

Cohen, Naomi W. *A Dual Heritage: The Public Career of Oscar S. Straus*, Phila., 1969.

_____. *Encounter With Emancipation: The German Jews In The United States 1830-1914*, Phila., 1984.

Commemoration of the One Hundredth Anniversary of the Birth of The Reverend Doctor Sabato Morais, Phila., 1924.

Davis, Edward. *The History of Rodeph Shalom Congregation, Philadelphia*, Phila., 1926.

Davis, Moshe. *The Emergence of Conservative Judaism: The Historical School in 19th Century America*, Phila., 1965.

_____. "Jewish Religious Life and Institutions in America (A Historical Study)," in *The Jews: Their Religion And Culture*, ed. Louis Finkelstein, N.Y., 1971, vol. 2, pp. 274-379.

_____. *Yahadut Amerika Be-hitpathutah (Toldot Haascola Hahistorit Bimayah Hatsha-esray)*, N.Y., 1951.

Dicker, Herman. *Of Learning And Libraries: The Seminary Library At One Hundred*, N.Y., 1988.

Eisenstein, Judah David. "The History of the First Russian-American Jewish Congregation," in *The Jewish Experience In America*, ed. Abraham J. Karp, N.Y./Waltham, 1969, vol. 3, pp. 140-151, reprinted from *PAJHS*, 1901.

Elbogen, Ismar. *A Century of Jewish Life*, trans. Moses Hadas, Phila. 1966.

Encyclopaedia Judaica, Jerusalem, 1973.

Fierstien, Robert E. "The Founding and Early Years of the Jewish Theological Seminary of America," *History of Higher Education Annual*, VII, 1987, pp. 69-78.

_____. "Solomon Schechter and the Zionist Movement," *Conservative Judaism*, XXIX, no. 3 (Spring, 1975) pp. 3-13.

Friesel, Evyatar. "The Age of Optimism in American Judaism, 1900-1920," in *A Bicentennial Festschrift for J.R. Marcus*, pp. 131-155.

Goldman, Israel M. "Henry W. Schneeberger: His Role in American Judaism," *AJHQ*, LVII, no. 2 (Dec., 1967), pp. 152-190.

Gottheil, Richard. *The Life of Gustav Gottheil; Memoir of a Priest in Israel*, Williamsport, Pa., 1930.

Greenberg, Simon. "The Jewish Theological Seminary of America, An Evaluation" reprinted from *Proceedings of the Rabbinical Assembly of America*, XXIV, 1960, pp. 114-153.

Grinstein, Hyman B. "Orthodox Judaism and Early Zionism in America," in *Early History of Zionism in America*, ed. Isidore S. Meyer, N.Y., 1958, pp. 219-227.

_____. *The Rise of the Jewish Community of New York: 1654-1860*, Phila., 1947.

Gurock, Jeffrey S. "Resisters and Accommodators: Varieties of Orthodox Rabbis in America, 1886-1983," *American Jewish Archives*, XXXV, no. 2 (Nov., 1983), pp. 100-187.

Harris, Isidore. "History of Jews' College," in *Jews' College Jubilee Volume*, London, 1906.

Hudson, Winthrop S. *Religion In America*, N.Y., 1965.

The Jewish Encyclopedia, N.Y., 1912.

The Jewish Theological Seminary of America, *Register*, 1977-1982.

Jick, Leon A. *The Americanization of the Synagogue 1820-1870*, Hanover, N.H., 1976.

Karp, Abraham J. "The Conservative Rabbi— 'Dissatisfied But Not Unhappy,'" in *The American Rabbinate: A Century of Continuity and Change: 1883-1983*, ed. Jacob Rader Marcus and Abraham J. Peck, Hoboken, 1985, pp. 98-172.

_____. "The Era of Immigration," in *The Jewish Experience In America*, vol. 4, pp. vii-xxi.

_____. *Haven and Home: A History of the Jews in America*, N.Y., 1985.

_____. "New York Chooses a Chief Rabbi," in *The Jewish Experience in America*, vol. 4, pp. 126-184, reprinted from *PAJHS*, 1954.

_____. "Solomon Schechter Comes to America," *AJHQ*, LII, no. 1 (Sept., 1963), pp. 42-62.

Kessner, Thomas. "Gershom Mendes Seixas: His Religious 'Calling,' Outlook and Competence," *AJHQ*, LVII, no. 4 (June, 1969), pp. 445-471.

Klaperman, Gilbert. *The Story of Yeshiva University: The First Jewish University in America*, no location given, 1969.

Kohut, George A. "A Memoir of Dr. Alexander Kohut's Literary Activity," in *Proceedings*, JTSA, 1894.

Korn, Bertram W. *American Jewry and the Civil War*, N.Y., 1970.

_____. *Eventful Years And Experiences: Studies in Nineteenth Century American Jewish History*, Cincinnati, 1954.

Markovitz, Eugene. *Henry Pereira Mendes (1877-1920)*, D.H.L. Dissertation, Yeshiva University, 1961.

_____. "Henry Pereira Mendes: Architect of the Union of Orthodox Jewish Congregations of America," *AJHQ*, LV, no. 3, (March, 1966), pp. 364-384.

May, Max B. *Isaac Mayer Wise: The Founder of American Judaism*, N.Y., 1916.

Meyer, Michael A. "A Centennial History," in *Hebrew Union College - Jewish Institute of Religion At One Hundred Years*, ed. Samuel E. Karff, no location given, 1976, pp. 1-283.

Morison , Samuel Eliot. *The Oxford History of the American People*, N.Y., 1965.

Nadell, Pamela S. *Conservative Judaism in America: A Biographical Dictionary and Sourcebook*, N.Y., 1988.

Nulman, Macy. *Concise Encyclopedia of Jewish Music*, N.Y., 1975.

Nussenbaum, Max Samuel. *Champion of Orthodox Judaism: A Biography of the Reverend Sabato Morais, LL.D., D.H.L.* Dissertation, Yeshiva University, 1964.

Parzen, Herbert. *Architects of Conservative Judaism*, N.Y., 1964.

_____. "The Federation of American Zionists (1897-1914)," in *Early History of Zionism in America*, pp. 245-274.

Plaut, W. Gunther. *The Rise of Reform Judaism: A Sourcebook of its European Origins*, N.Y., 1963.

de Sola Pool, David and Tamar. *An Old Faith in the New World: Portrait of Shearith Israel, 1654-1954*, N.Y., 1955.

Price, George M. "The Russian Jews in America," translator Leo Shpall, in *The Jewish Experience in America*, vol. 4, pp. 265-355, reprinted from *PAJHS*, 1958.

Raphael, Marc Lee. *Profiles in American Judaism: The Reform, Conservative, Orthodox, and Reconstructionist Traditions in Historical Perspective*, San Francisco, 1984.

Rischin, Moses. *The Promised City: New York's Jews 1870-1914*, N.Y., 1970.

Rosenblum, Herbert. *Conservative Judaism: A Contemporary History*, N.Y., 1983.

_____. *The Founding of the United Synagogue of America, 1913*, Ph.D. dissertation, Brandeis University, 1970.

_____. "The Shaping of an Institution: The 1902 Reorganization of the Seminary," *Conservative Judaism*, XXVII, no. 2 (Winter, 1973), pp. 35-48.

Rothkoff, Aaron. *Bernard Revel, Builder of American Jewish Orthodoxy*, Philadelphia, 1972.

Schorsch, Ismar, "Ideology and History in the Age of Emancipation," in Heinrich Graetz, *The Structure of Jewish History*, ed. and translator Ismar Schorsch, N.Y., 1975.

_____. "Zacharias Frankel and the European Origins of Conservative Judaism," *Judaism*, vol. 30, no. 3 (Summer, 1981), pp. 344-354.

The Universal Jewish Encyclopedia, N.Y., 1941.

Vorspan, Max, and Lloyd P. Gartner. *History of the Jews of Los Angeles*, San Marino, Calif., 1970.

Waxman, Mordecai. "Conservative Judaism—A Survey," in *Tradition And Change: The Development of Conservative Judaism*, ed. Mordecai Waxman, N.Y., 1958.

Wertheimer, Jack, ed. *The American Synagogue: A Sanctuary Transformed*, N.Y., 1987.

_____. "The Conservative Synagogue Revisited," *AJH*, LXXIV, no. 2 (Dec., 1984), pp. 118-132.

Whiteman, Maxwell. "Isaac Leeser and the Jews of Philadelphia," in *The Jewish Experience in America*, Vol. 3, pp. 27-62, reprinted from *PAJHS*, 1959.

_____. "Zionism Comes To Philadelphia," in *Early History of Zionism in America*, pp. 191-218.

Zola, Gary P. "Reform Judaism's Pioneer Zionist: Maximilian Heller," *AJH*, LXXIII, no. 4 (June, 1984), pp. 375-397.